CHARLES DICKENS
THE WRITER AND HIS WORK

CHARLES DICKENS
THE WRITER AND HIS WORK

Selected and Edited by
M. AND P. FLOYD

Biography Index Reprint Series

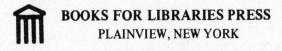
BOOKS FOR LIBRARIES PRESS
PLAINVIEW, NEW YORK

Reprinted 1975 by arrangement
with Lonmans,Green Limited.

Dickens, Charles, 1812-1870.
Charles Dickens: the writer and his work.

(Biography index reprint series)
Reprint of the 1948 ed. published by
Longmans Green London in series:
Essencial English Library.
I. Floyd, M., ed. II. Floyd,P., ed. III.Title.
IV. Series: Essencial English Library.
PR4552.F5   823'.8   74-920
ISBN 0-8369-8196-0

PRINTED IN THE UNITED STATES OF AMERICA

Editor's Preface

*

THE Essential English Library is a series of books some fiction, some non-fiction, intended mainly for foreign students, though it is hoped that English readers may also find them of interest. The fiction has been chosen from some of the best writers, old and new, of English novels, short stories and plays. The non-fiction consists mainly of completely new books specially written by experts for this series, on various aspects of English life and institutions.

The books are meant for serious adult students, and, though the vocabulary is carefully controlled, the style is natural and vigorous, and there is no question of any childish "writing down." The vocabulary is fundamentally that of the four books of *Essential English*. But, to widen the students' knowledge of the language, the same principle has been adopted in this series as in the later books of *Essential English*. So a number of new words (averaging three or four to a page) occur in each volume, but every new word is given, with the phonetic transcription, in the Glossary at the end of the book, and each word in the Glossary is defined within the vocabulary of *Essential English*.

All the books are about the same length, and are illustrated with photographs or line drawings.

The general editor will welcome suggestions for additions to the series.

C. E. E.

Contents

ACKNOWLEDGMENTS

The letter from Dickens and the page from the MS. of *Nicholas Nickleby* are reproduced by kind permission of the Trustees of The Dickens House, 48 Doughty Street, London, W.C.1.

6

Introduction

IT is doubtful whether any English writer has ever been so popular as Dickens was in his lifetime, popular not only with one class or one generation, but with all classes, rich and poor, young and old alike. When *Pickwick Papers* came out, Lord Chief Justice Campbell said he would be prouder of having written that book than of all the honours he had earned at the Bar. Lord Carlisle said, "Dickens is the master of our sunniest smile and our most unselfish tear." Maurois tells a charming story of a small boy who, hearing in 1870 of Dickens's death, said, "Mr. Dickens dead! And will Father Christmas die too?" Thomas Carlyle was told by a clergyman that a dying man whom he had been visiting had murmured as the clergyman left the room, "Well, thank God, the next instalment of *Pickwick* will be out in ten days, anyway." When Dickens was buried in Westminster Abbey, close by the monuments to Chaucer, Shakespeare, and Dryden, there was a constant stream of mourners for days. "All day long," wrote Dean Stanley, "crowds passed slowly by; many flowers were laid there by unknown hands, many tears shed from unknown eyes."* And to this day the names of Pickwick and Sam Weller, Oliver Twist, Squeers, Mr. Micawber, Fagin, Mrs. Gamp, and a host of others are household words in England, familiar as are no other characters in the whole of English literature.

Nor was Dickens's fame confined only to England. Dickens himself had none of the insularity that was then, and to some extent still is, an English characteristic. He spent much of his time abroad, and spoke French and Italian well. When he visited America, he was cheered by big crowds in the streets, and welcomed by politicians, judges, and bishops; dinners everywhere were planned in his honour; theatre audiences rose at his entrance, and he was so overwhelmed

* Slightly adapted into *Essential English*.

7

with letters, invitations, flowers, gifts, offers of hospitality, and requests for lectures and interviews that he had to engage a secretary to deal with them all.* In Russia, Tolstoy condemned Parliamentary government because Dickens did not favour it. In Germany, Moltke and his officers based their opinion of English character on Dickens's books, and on his death an Italian paper had for its headlines, "Il nostro Carlo Dickens è morto"(*Our* Charles Dickens is dead).

But if Dickens was not insular, he was essentially English and Victorian. His age was an age of transition—the Industrial Revolution was rapidly gaining power, and England was changing from a country that was mainly agricultural to a country that was mainly industrial. But Dickens knew only imperfectly the industrial classes of the Midlands and the North. There, machinery was coming into all the mills, life was getting harder and more dreary for working people. Vast wealth went side by side with grinding poverty, wretchedness, and misery. But this is not the England that Dickens depicts. Though the steam-engine appeared in 1830 (when Dickens was eighteen), his England was mainly an England of the stage-coach. This was the England that he loved, the plain, homely, old-fashioned England of country inns, of queer old shops and little houses comfortable in the vastness of the city. And of this he draws picture after picture, his genius playing on it in a warm light. Not that he doesn't see the misery there too. He knew that only too well. He could reveal the poor of England to the wealthy because he had known the hardship of poverty; he could make the wealthy and the powerful listen to his championing of the poor because (though he became a wealthy landed owner himself) he could never forget—or ever desired to forget—an unhappy childhood in London.

He was born in Portsea, a part of Portsmouth, on February 7th, 1812. His father, John Dickens, was a clerk in the Navy Pay Office, a cheerful happy-go-lucky fellow who told good

* His popularity, however, declined for a time when he, perhaps somewhat unwisely, criticised American "democracy" and their unfair treatment of copyright.

Introduction

stories, was very willing to entertain the world at his house,
lived beyond his income, and, like Mr. Micawber (of whom
he was the model), always hoped that "something would turn
up." Generally it didn't. Debts grew heavier. The Dickens
family moved from Portsmouth to Chatham, and then, when
Charles was eleven, to London. Here things went from bad
to worse. At Chatham, Charles had been at the school of a
Mr. Giles, who had recognised something of the boy's quick
intelligence and had encouraged his taste for reading. Not
that it needed much encouragement. In one of the top rooms
of the house he found a collection of books that his father
had bought at some time or other—*Robinson Crusoe*,* *Tom
Jones*,† *The Vicar of Wakefield*,‡ *Arabian Nights*, and,
above all, *Don Quixote*.§ Hard reading for a boy of ten, but
Charles devoured them eagerly. He read and re-read them,
and they opened up to him an endless treasure of adventure
and romance.

When he came to London, there was apparently to be no
more schooling for him. His father's debts were growing.
One by one their possessions, even the books, were sold. Mrs.
Dickens had the wild idea of opening a private school. A
brass plate was put on the front door inscribed "School for
Young Ladies. Mrs. Dickens." Charles and his brothers and
sisters were sent round the neighbourhood pushing handbills
through the letter-boxes, but no pupils came to the school.
When things looked darkest, a relative of the family, Mr.
Lamert, offered Charles, now aged twelve, work in his blacking factory on the Thames by Hungerford Bridge, at six
shillings a week. To the end of his life Dickens never lost the
memory of the unhappiness, the humiliation, that he felt
during this time. So bitter was it that for years he could
never bear to speak of it. Meanwhile John Dickens had been
arrested for debt, and he and his family were taken to the
Marshalsea Prison, where Charles visited them every day.

* By Daniel Defoe (1661–1731).
† By Henry Fielding (1707–1754).
‡ By Oliver Goldsmith (1728–1774).
§ By the great Spanish writer Cervantes (1547–1616).

9

But now the tide began to turn. A small legacy rescued Mr. Dickens from prison. He got a job as Parliamentary reporter for a newspaper, *The British Press*, and he took Charles away from the blacking factory and gave him another year or two at school, this time at Mr. Jones's "Classical and Commercial Academy," where the boy was happy enough, though as he said later, "The place was most shamefully mismanaged and the boys made little progress."

Before he was sixteen he was working as a clerk in a lawyer's office. For ten and sixpence, his whole savings, he bought a book on shorthand, and began to teach himself. After much effort (he describes the struggle vividly in *David Copperfield*), he became an excellent shorthand writer, and after serving some time as a reporter at the law courts, he became a reporter on the newspaper *True Sun*. His work here gave him invaluable experience. He travelled about England, reporting meetings and events, seeing all kinds of people, gathering the material that he used so brilliantly later.

At the age of twenty-one, "with fear and trembling," he sent a short story signed by the name "Boz" to a magazine. To his delight the editor accepted it (though he didn't offer to pay the author anything for it) and asked for more. Dickens gladly sent more, and in 1836 the stories were collected into a volume, *Sketches by Boz*. The book was a success, and many people began asking who "Boz" was. About Christmas, 1836, Mr. Hall, a partner in the publishing firm of Chapman & Hall, came to see Dickens, with the suggestion that the latter should write some sketches for a series of illustrations that the well-known comic artist Robert Seymour was doing for them. The work was intended to be a joke at the expense of Cockney "sportsmen," who hardly knew one end of a gun from the other and who would be shown falling on the ice or off their horses. The work would appear in twenty monthly parts, published at a shilling. Dickens didn't quite like the idea. He knew nothing of sport, and would have preferred to write the sketches and let Seymour illustrate them. But he was planning to be married, the money was tempting

Introduction

(£25 per number), so Dickens accepted the offer—and *Pick-wick Papers* was born. The first two numbers were not very well received, and at this point Seymour shot himself. The sales, indeed, had been so poor that the publishers hesitated about continuing the series. However, they decided to go on with it, and various other artists were suggested (including Thackeray). But in the end Hablot K. Brown ("Phiz") was chosen, and so began the happy partnership of "Boz" and "Phiz." The work still sold very slowly (about 400 copies each month) until, in the fifth number, Dickens introduced Sam Weller. The success was instantaneous and overwhelming. The sales leapt up in no time from 400 to 40,000. The country went Pickwick mad. People named their cats and dogs "Pickwick," "Sam," "Boz," or "Jingle." There were Pickwick hats, Pickwick coats, and Weller trousers. "Boz" cabs appeared on the streets. Ladies used "Pickwick" perfume and men smoked "Pickwick" cigars. At twenty-four Dickens had become, and for the rest of his life remained, the most famous of English novelists. At a later period of his life Dickens planned his novels and worked out his complicated plots. In *Pickwick Papers* there is no plan. Dickens just "thought of Pickwick," pushed him and the rest of the characters into the world—and followed them. The story grew as it went along. So, too, did the characters, especially Mr. Pickwick. Dickens had begun by making him merely a comic figure. But he mellows and becomes a lovable figure, an English Don Quixote (attended by an equally English Sancho Panza, Sam Weller), kindly, sentimental, shining with good humour, but full of common sense, and with an English obstinacy when he felt that he was in the right that endeared him to all his countrymen. And all the Pickwickian adventures were against a background of England that its readers loved, a rural England of stage-coaches, of jolly Christmas eating and drinking, of warm fires, good fellowship, and simple-hearted pleasures.

While Pickwick was still running, Dickens was already at work on his next book, *Oliver Twist*, and in 1838 the first number appeared in *Bentley's Magazine*. But despite the fact that it appeared in instalments,* as Pickwick had done, the method of writing was different. This book was not a loosely connected series of adventures; Dickens was now building a novel with a carefully worked-out plot. Its story was of a sensitive child suffering from the cruelties of the workhouse. He escapes from there only to face Fagin's den of thieves and the miseries of a police-court and a lock-up cell.

The popularity of *Oliver Twist* surpassed even that of *Pickwick Papers,* and not the less because Dickens was no longer merely amusing his public but was lighting up dark places that his comfortable, well-to-do readers didn't know existed or hadn't troubled to investigate. A reviewer † of the day wrote, "Life in London as revealed in the pages of *Oliver Twist* opens a new world to thousands born and bred in the same city whose palaces overshadow these cellars—for the one half of mankind lives without knowing how the other half dies."

Dickens always considered himself as much a social reformer as a novelist, and the noble indignation that he had felt in *Oliver Twist* burns even more fiercely in his next work, *Nicholas Nickleby,* the first numbers of which appeared in 1839, while *Oliver Twist* was still running. Here his attack was on the cruel treatment of "unwanted" children in certain private schools. Dickens tells us that he first began to think of these schools when, as a child, he met a boy who had been unhappy in one of them. They were still flourishing, especially in Yorkshire, when Dickens was a man. He had had them in mind for some time, and just after Christmas, 1837, he wrote to his friend Harrison Ainsworth,‡ "I start on my journey to the cheap schools of Yorkshire (a mighty secret of course) next Monday morning." So that his purpose would not be known, he visited them under an assumed name, with the excuse that he was acting for a widowed friend who wanted to put her two boys into a

---

* All Dickens's books appeared originally in monthly instalments.
† Richard Ford.
‡ Well-known English novelist (1805–1882). Author of *The Tower of London, Old St. Paul's,* etc.

school. What he saw there stung him to action. He hurried back to London and plunged into the writing of *Nicholas Nickleby*. The success of the book was enormous—50,000 copies of the first instalment were sold on the first day—and

Charles Dickens as a young man
(from the portrait by Maclise)

the storm caused by Mr. Squeers and the Yorkshire schools was even fiercer than that caused by Mr. Bumble and the workhouses.

Dickens was now at the height of his fame and the height of his activity, mental and physical. He thought nothing of a twenty-mile walk, and would not be put off it by rain or snow. His creative power always was enormous. He edited papers, wrote novels and sketches, lectured, travelled, produced plays, and gave public readings of his work. Even his face, as Leigh Hunt * said, "had the life and soul in it of fifty human beings." In 1840 came *The Old Curiosity Shop*, in 1841 *Barnaby Rudge*. After a visit to America, he wrote *American Notes* and *Martin Chuzzlewit*. In 1843 and the two succeeding Christmases, he won new popularity with his "Christmas Books"—*A Christmas Carol*, *The Chimes*, and *The Cricket on the Hearth*. Then followed *Dombey and Son*, and in 1850, what is generally regarded as his masterpiece, the largely autobiographical *David Copperfield*. Between 1853 and 1870 he wrote *Bleak House, Hard Times, Little Dorrit, A Tale of Two Cities, Great Expectations*, and *Our Mutual Friend*. But the strain was telling heavily. He was quite incapable of resting. Years before, he had said to his friend and first biographer, Forster, "I am quite confident I should rust, break, and die if I spared myself." He certainly did not spare himself. To the strain of writing was now added the strain of public readings from his books in England and America, and these readings in his earlier years took a great deal out of Dickens and certainly hastened his death. He couldn't sleep at night, could hardly eat solid food, and could only get energy enough for the readings in the evenings by resting all day.

In 1870 the first number of *The Mystery of Edwin Drood* appeared; but this book was never to be finished. On June 8th, as he was at dinner, he became seriously ill, and twenty-four hours later, at the age of fifty-eight, he died.

What is the secret of Dickens's greatness? What were his qualities? What his achievements? Our attention in this present volume is directed only to the first three of Dickens's books; but these books illustrate perfectly almost all his characteristics. Outstanding in at least two of them is, of course, Dickens the social reformer. That was how his own generation regarded him. "Charles Dickens," said Daniel

---

* Leigh Hunt (1784–1859), essayist, editor, and poet.

Introduction

Webster,* has done more to improve the conditions of the English poor than all the statesmen that Great Britain has sent to Parliament." Dickens himself said, "By literature I have lived, and through literature I have been content to serve my country. . . . I have tried to understand the heavier social grievances and to help to set them right," a point of view which links him up with a whole group of writers of the time, for example, Disraeli, Bulwer Lytton, Kingsley, Mrs. Gaskell, and Charlotte Brontë. But the vital difference between their approach and his is that they had never known in their own lives what it meant as a child to want food and the security of home life; what it meant to desire education passionately and to be condemned to labour at work that they hated. They wrote sympathetically about the poor because they understood imaginatively the troubles of the poor. Dickens wrote burningly because he had been one of them. The unforgettable experiences of his childhood were a decisive element in Dickens's whole life. It is with suffering children that he is most associated; it was in this direction that his influence for reform was as great as any.

The intensity of feeling for the oppressed was the mainspring of his whole social philosophy. Not that he ever formulated any social philosophy. True, he hated the cruelties of the workhouse system, of the private schools, the debtors' prisons, the law's delays. He would abolish all these. But he had no idea what should take their places. He hated reformist theories. He disliked legislation generally, and was bitter in his attacks on Parliamentary government. He didn't believe that the poor could be made happier by any Acts of Parliament or by organised charity. He hated organised charity, despite the fact that he gave speeches for children's hospitals, homes for artists, charities for newspaper sellers, gardeners, railwaymen, clerks, and a host of others. It was the soullessness of organised charity that he disliked, the charity that carried for the receiver a mark of disgrace. He wanted a change of heart, not a change of social system. His only remedy for the hated educational system, however, was kinder

* Daniel Webster (1782–1852), American statesman and writer.

15

schoolmasters. His social reform consists of private benevolence by smiling, rosy-cheeked, elderly gentlemen (like Mr.
Pickwick or the Cheeryble brothers), men with kind hearts
and large fortunes who do all the good they can, smiling and
rubbing their hands with pleasure as they do it. Their action
is domestic and narrow, because if it were wider it might be
in danger of becoming political. Their symbol is Christmas;
their philosophy human kindness.

His religious ideas are equally simple. He sums them up
in a letter he wrote to his son Edward when the latter was
going to Australia.

"Never take a mean advantage of anyone . . . and never be
hard upon people who are in your power. Try to do to others
as you would have them do to you, and do not be discouraged
if they fail sometimes. It is much better that they should fail
in obeying the greatest rule laid down by Christ than that
you should. . . .

"Never abandon the wholesome practice of saying your
own private prayers, night and morning. I have never aban-
doned it myself, and I know the comfort of it."

In his will he left this message to his children, "Guide
yourself by the teachings of the New Testament in its broad
spirit, and put no faith in any man's narrow construction of
its letter here and there." That is the essence of his religion.

In his fight to rouse sympathy on behalf of sufferers of all
classes, Dickens possessed the weapon of humour. "He could
make the people laugh; and if once the crowd has laughed
with you it will not object to cry a little—nay, it will make
good resolves and sometimes carry them out. Only because
they laughed with him so heartily did people turn to discussing the question his pages suggested."* Nineteenth-
century England was very proud of its "progress." It would
not have endured patiently violent attacks against the institutions it so much admired—but it read *Oliver Twist* and
Nicholas Nickleby, and laughed and cried over them. For
the humour of Dickens is not the dry bitter humour that
comes from the lips only; it comes from the heart. Nor is it

* From *Charles Dickens*, by George Gissing (1898).

merely the broad humour of comic situation (though Dickens had that form of humour too); it is deep-rooted in character; it throws light on human nature, and over it all shines the light of true charity, so that he sees even Bumble or Mrs. Gamp or Squeers with that large tolerance that is the spirit of Chaucer and Shakespeare and Cervantes and all the supreme humorists.

He is like Shakespeare, too, in the marvellous creative power of his mind, the creation of men and women on paper who are in many ways more real to us than the friends who surround us; characters who are as unusual and eccentric as Squeers, Weller, Pecksniff, and Micawber, yet as universal as human nature. The accusation is often brought against Dickens that he doesn't create "characters" but "caricatures"; that his people are not real individuals, but creatures observed only from the outside, with a single constantly repeated mannerism. Thus Mr. Micawber is always "waiting for something to turn up"; Uriah Heep has cold, damp hands and is "humble"; Sam Weller makes humorous comparisons; Mrs. Squeers is always giving boys brimstone; Mrs. Gummidge always weeping. Perhaps. But the undoubted fact is that they all *live*; that is his supreme achievement. And they live by the power of imagination with which Dickens almost overwhelms them, the realistic details that he gives us that force us to believe the incredible. Mr. Squeers, for example, makes a speech to the boys, and we learn that Bolder's father was £2 10s. 0d. short; that Cobbey's Uncle John has taken to drink. Cobbey's sister sends eighteenpence which will pay for a broken window. Graymarsh's aunt would have sent two pairs of stockings, but is short of money so sends a Bible lesson instead, and hopes Graymarsh will put his trust in God and won't object to sleeping five in a bed. Mobbs's stepmother had to go to her bed on hearing Mobbs wouldn't eat fat.* Who could disbelieve in the reality of Squeers, after that? The reason we believe in them is, of course, that Dickens believes intensely in his characters himself. "I am certain," said Dickens's son

* See page 91.

Charley, "that the children of my father's brain were much more to him than we were." "Dickens said that he could never entirely dismiss the characters about whom he happened to be writing, that while *The Old Curiosity Shop* was being written Little Nell followed him everywhere, that while he wrote *Oliver Twist* Fagin would never let him rest."* When he wrote the scene of the death of Little Nell, Dickens says, "I was obliged to lock myself in when I had finished it yesterday for my face was swollen with crying." And in the preface to *David Copperfield* he writes, "It would interest the reader little, perhaps, to know how sorrowfully the pen is laid down at the end of a two years' imaginative task; or how an author feels as if he were dismissing some part of himself into the shadowy world when a crowd of all the creatures of his brain are going from him for ever. Yet I had nothing else to tell unless indeed I were to confess . . . that no one can ever believe this story in the reading more than I believed it in the writing." †

There is the secret of Dickens's power. It lies in his sincerity, his creative imagination, his humanity. He understood the lives, the joys, and the sorrows of simple folk of England as perhaps no other writer has ever done; and the simple folk of England will keep his memory green.

C. E. ECKERSLEY.

* *Life of Charles Dickens,* by John Forster (1812–76)
† Slightly adapted into *Essential English.*

BARDELL AND PICKWICK
(from *Pickwick Papers*)

I

[Mr. Tupman, Mr. Snodgrass, and Mr. Winkle are members of the Pickwick Club, of which Mr. Pickwick is the respected leader. The following is one of their many adventures.]

MR. PICKWICK'S rooms in Goswell Street, although on a limited scale, were not only of a very neat and comfortable description, but peculiarly adapted for the residence of a man of his genius and observation. His sitting-room was the first-floor, his bedroom the second-floor in the front; and thus, whether he was sitting at his desk in his sitting-room or standing before the looking-glass in his bedroom, he had an equal opportunity of studying human nature in all the numerous aspects it exhibits, in that populous and popular street. His landlady, Mrs. Bardell—the widow of a custom-house officer—was a good-looking woman of energetic manners and agreeable appearance, with a natural genius for cooking, improved by study and long practice into a fine art. There were no children, no servants, no chickens. The only other people in the house were a large man and a small boy; the first a lodger, the second a production of Mrs. Bardell's. The large man was always home precisely at ten o'clock at night, at which hour he regularly condensed himself into the limits of a small bed in the back room; and the childish sports and exercises of Master Bardell were without exception carried on in the neighbouring streets. Cleanliness and quiet reigned throughout the house; and in it Mr. Pickwick's will was law.

To anyone familiar with these points of the domestic habits of the establishment, and knowing the admirable regulation of Mr. Pickwick's mind, his appearance and behaviour on the morning previous to that which had been fixed upon for the journey to Eatanswill would have been most mysterious and unusual. He walked up and down the room with hurried steps, put his head out of the window at intervals of about three minutes each, constantly referred to his watch, and exhibited many other signs of impatience very unusual with him. It was evident that something of great importance was in mind, but what that something was not even Mrs. Bardell herself had been able to discover.

"Mrs. Bardell," said Mr. Pickwick at last, as that amiable female approached the end of a long-drawn-out dusting of the room.

"Sir," said Mrs. Bardell.

"Your little boy has been away a long time."

"Why, it's a good long way to the Borough, sir," protested Mrs. Bardell.

"Ah," said Mr. Pickwick, "very true; so it is."

Mr. Pickwick said no more, and Mrs. Bardell continued her dusting.

"Mrs. Bardell," said Mr. Pickwick at the end of a few minutes.

"Sir," said Mrs. Bardell again.

"Do you think it is a much greater expense to keep two people than to keep one?"

"Oh! Mr. Pickwick," said Mrs. Bardell, colouring up to the very border of her cap, as she fancied she observed a kind of matrimonial twinkle in the eyes of her lodger; "Mr. Pickwick, what a question!"

"Well, but do you?" inquired Mr. Pickwick.

"That depends," said Mrs. Bardell, studying the duster very near to Mr. Pickwick's elbow, which was resting on the table—"that depends a good deal upon the person; you know, Mr. Pickwick; and whether it's a saving and careful person, sir."

"That's very true," said Mr. Pickwick, "but the person I have in my eye" (here he looked very hard at Mrs. Bardell), "I think possesses these qualities; and has, in addition, a considerable knowledge of the world, and a great deal of sharpness, Mrs. Bardell, which may be of great use to me."

"Oh! Mr. Pickwick," said Mrs. Bardell, the blushes rising to her cap-border again.

"I do," said Mr. Pickwick, growing energetic, as was his

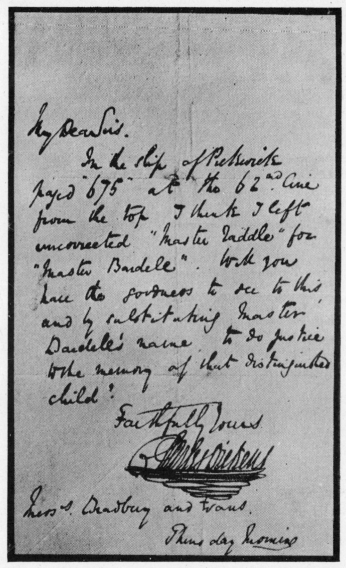

A letter from Dickens to his publishers about Pickwick Papers

custom in speaking of a subject which interested him—"I do, indeed; and to tell the truth, Mrs. Bardell, I have made up my mind."

"Dear me, sir!" exclaimed Mrs. Bardell.

"You'll think it very strange now," said the amiable Mr. Pickwick, with a good-humoured glance at his companion, "that I never consulted you about this matter, and never even mentioned it, till I sent your boy out this morning—eh?"

Mrs. Bardell could only reply by a look. She had long worshipped Mr. Pickwick at a distance, but here she was, all at once, raised to a peak which her wildest hopes had never dared to reach. Mr. Pickwick was going to propose—a deliberate plan, too—sent her little boy to the Borough, to get him out of the way—how thoughtful—how considerate!

"Well," said Mr. Pickwick, "what do you think?"

"Oh, Mr. Pickwick," said Mrs. Bardell, trembling with agitation, "you're very kind, sir."

"It'll save you a good deal of trouble, won't it?" said Mr. Pickwick.

"Oh, I never thought anything of the trouble, sir," replied Mrs. Bardell; "and of course, I should take more trouble to please you then than ever; but it is so kind of you, Mr. Pickwick, to have so much consideration for my loneliness."

"Ah, to be sure," said Mr. Pickwick, "I never thought of that. When I am in London, you'll always have somebody to sit with you. To be sure, so you will."

"I am sure I ought to be a very happy woman," said Mrs. Bardell.

"And your little boy——" said Mr. Pickwick.

"Bless his heart!" interrupted Mrs. Bardell with a mother's sob.

"He, too, will have a companion," continued Mr. Pickwick, "a lively one, who'll teach him, I'm sure, more tricks in a week than he would ever learn in a year."

"Oh, you dear——" said Mrs. Bardell.

Mr. Pickwick started.

"Oh, you kind, good, playful dear," said Mrs. Bardell.

And without saying any more, she rose from her chair, and flung her arms round Mr. Pickwick's neck, with a flood of tears and a chorus of sobs.

"Bless my soul," cried the astonished Mr. Pickwick. "Mrs. Bardell, my good woman—dear me, what a situation—please consider,—Mrs. Bardell, don't—if anybody should come——"

"Oh, let them come," exclaimed Mrs. Bardell hysterically; "I'll never leave you—dear, kind, good soul"; and, with these words Mrs. Bardell clung the tighter.

"Mercy upon me," said Mr. Pickwick, struggling violently, "I hear somebody coming up the stairs. Don't, don't, there's a good creature, don't." But prayers and protests were alike useless; for Mrs. Bardell had fainted in Mr. Pickwick's arms; and before he could gain time to place her on a chair, Master Bardell entered the room, showing in Mr. Tupman, Mr. Winkle, and Mr. Snodgrass.

Mr. Pickwick was struck motionless and speechless. He stood with his lovely burden in his arms, gazing stupidly at the faces of his friends, without the slightest attempt at recognition or explanation. They, in their turn, stared at him; and Master Bardell, in his turn, stared at everybody.

The astonishment of the Pickwickians was so absorbing, and the embarrassment of Mr. Pickwick was so extreme, that they might have remained in exactly the same relative situations until the recovery of the lady, if it had not been for a most beautiful and touching expression of affection on the part of her youthful son. Clad in a tight suit, with brass buttons of a very considerable size, he at first stood at the door astounded and uncertain; but by degrees, the impression that his mother must have suffered some personal damage dawned on his partially developed mind, and considering Mr. Pickwick as the enemy, he set up an awful and semi-earthly kind of howling, and running forward with his head lowered, began to attack that immortal gentleman about the back and legs, with such blows and pinches as the strength of his arm, and the violence of his excitement, allowed.

"Take this little villain away," said the agonised Mr. Pickwick; "he's mad."

"What is the matter?" said the three tongue-tied Pickwickians.

"I don't know," replied Mr. Pickwick irritably. "Take away the boy." (Here Mr. Winkle carried the boy, screaming and struggling, to the farther end of the room.) "Now help me lead this woman downstairs."

"Oh, I am better now," said Mrs. Bardell faintly.

"Let me lead you downstairs," said the ever-gallant Mr. Tupman.

And downstairs she was led accordingly, accompanied by her affectionate son.

"I cannot imagine," said Mr. Pickwick when his friend returned; "I cannot imagine what has been the matter with that woman. I merely announced to her my intention of keeping a man-servant, when she fell into the extraordinary condition in which you found her. Very extraordinary thing."

"Very," said his three friends.

"Placed me in such an extremely awkward situation," continued Mr. Pickwick.

"Very," was the reply of his followers, as they coughed slightly and looked doubtfully at each other.

This behaviour was not lost upon Mr. Pickwick. He noticed their incredulity. They evidently suspected him.

"There is a man just outside now," said Mr. Tupman.

"It's the man I spoke to you about," said Mr. Pickwick; "I sent for him to the Borough this morning. Have the goodness to call him up, Snodgrass."

Mr. Snodgrass did as he was desired; and Mr. Samuel Weller immediately presented himself.

"Oh—you remember me, I suppose?" said Mr. Pickwick. "Sit down."

"Thank you, sir," said Sam. And down he sat without further asking, having previously placed his old white hat outside the door.

"Now with regard to the matter on which I, with the

agreement of these gentlemen, sent for you," said Mr. Pickwick.

"That's the point, sir," interrupted Sam; "out with it, as the father said to his child, when he swallowed a farthing."

"We want to know, in the first place," said Mr. Pickwick, "whether you have any reason to be discontented with your present situation."

"Before I answer that question, gentlemen," replied Mr. Weller, "I should like to know, in the first place, whether you're going to provide me with a better one."

Mr. Pickwick smiled amiably as he said, "I have half made up my mind to engage you myself."

"Have you, though?" said Sam.

Mr. Pickwick nodded.

"Wages?" inquired Sam.

"Twelve pounds a year," replied Mr. Pickwick.

"Clothes?"

"Two suits."

"Work?"

"To wait on me; and travel about with me and these gentlemen here."

"Take the notice down," said Sam emphatically. "I'm let to a single gentleman, and the terms are agreed upon."

"You accept the situation?" inquired Mr. Pickwick.

"Certainly," replied Sam. "If the clothes fit me half as well as the place, they'll do."

"You can get a reference of character, of course?" said Mr. Pickwick.

"Ask the landlady of the White Hart about that, sir," replied Sam.

"Can you come this evening?"

"I'll get into the clothes this minute, if they're here," said Sam quickly.

"Call at eight this evening," said Mr. Pickwick, "and if the inquiries are satisfactory, they shall be provided."

The history of Mr. Weller's conduct was so very blameless that Mr. Pickwick felt justified in closing the engagement that very evening; and before night, Mr. Weller was provided with a grey coat with buttons, a black hat with a feather in it, a pink waistcoat, tight trousers, and a variety of other necessaries too numerous to mention.

II

[Later, the Pickwickians meet together in the country. They have been the victims of several unfortunate incidents, and their leader is expressing his fear that the club's reputation may be suffering.]

"Is it not a wonderful circumstance," said Mr. Pickwick, "that we never seem to enter any man's house without involving him in some degree of trouble? Does it not, I ask, show the foolishness or, worse than that, the blackness of heart—that I should say so!—of my followers, that, beneath whatever roof they stay, they disturb the peace of mind and happiness of some trusting female? Is it not, I say——"

Mr. Pickwick would in all probability have gone on for some time had not the entrance of Sam, with a letter, caused him to break off his eloquent speech. He passed his handkerchief across his forehead, took off his glasses, wiped them, and put them on again; and his voice had recovered its usual softness when he said:

"What have you there, Sam?"

"I called at the post-office just now, and found this letter, which has lain there for two days," replied Mr. Weller. "It's sealed, and addressed in hand-writing."

"I don't know this hand," said Mr. Pickwick, opening the letter. "Mercy on us! What's this? It must be a joke. It—it—can't be true."

"What's the matter?" was the general inquiry.

Mr. Pickwick made no reply, but, pushing the letter across the table, and desiring Mr. Tupman to read it aloud, fell back in his chair with a look of complete astonishment, quite alarming to see.

Mr. Tupman, with a trembling voice, read the letter, of which the following is a copy:

Bardell and Pickwick

Freeman's Court, Cornhill.
August 28th, 1830.
Bardell against Pickwick.

Sir,

Having been instructed by Mrs. Martha Bardell to begin an action at law against you for breach of promise of marriage, for which the plaintiff claims damages of fifteen hundred pounds, we beg to inform you that proceedings have been taken against you in this case; and request to know, by return of post, the name of your lawyer in London, who will defend you.

We are, Sir,
Your obedient servants,
Dodson & Fogg.

Mr. Samuel Pickwick.

There was something so impressive in the speechless astonishment with which each man regarded his neighbour, and every man regarded Mr. Pickwick, that all seemed afraid to speak. The silence was at last broken by Mr. Tupman.

"Dodson and Fogg," he repeated mechanically.

"Bardell and Pickwick," said Mr. Snodgrass thoughtfully.

"Peace of mind and happiness of trusting females," murmured Mr. Winkle dreamily.

"It's a plot," said Mr. Pickwick, at length recovering the power of speech "a low-down plot between these two greedy lawyers, Dodson and Fogg. Mrs. Bardell would never do it —she has no case at all. Ridiculous—ridiculous. It's a mean attempt to get money," he continued with great emphasis. "Whoever heard me speak to her in any way but that in which a lodger would speak to a landlady? Whoever saw me with her? Not even my friends here——"

"Except on one occasion," said Mr. Tupman.

Mr. Pickwick changed colour.

Mr. Tupman glanced timidly at his leader. "There was nothing suspicious," said he, "but—I don't know how it happened, mind—she certainly was lying in his arms."

"Good heavens!" cried Mr. Pickwick as the remembrance

of the scene in question struck him forcibly; "what an awful instance of the force of circumstances! So she was—so she was."

"And our friend was comforting her," said Mr. Winkle, rather spitefully.

"So I was," said Mr. Pickwick. "I don't deny it. So I was. What an awful combination of appearances! Winkle—Tupman—I beg your pardon for the remarks I made just now. We are all the victims of circumstances, and I the greatest." With this apology Mr. Pickwick buried his head in his hands, and thought hard, "I'll have it explained, though," he continued, raising his head and hammering the table. "I'll see this Dodson and Fogg! I'll go to London to-morrow."

III

[Several months have passed. Mr. Pickwick's efforts to settle the affair out of court have failed, and we find him with his friends and his lawyer, Mr. Perker, gathered together on the day of the trial.]

"I wonder what the foreman, whoever he'll be, has got for breakfast," said Mr. Snodgrass, by way of keeping up a conversation on the eventful morning of the fourteenth of February.

"Ah!" said Mr. Perker, Mr. Pickwick's lawyer, "I hope he's got a good one."

"Why?" inquired Mr. Pickwick.

"Highly important—very important, my dear sir," replied Perker. "A good, contented, well-breakfasted juryman is an excellent thing to get hold of."

"Ten minutes past nine!" said the little man, looking at his watch. "Time we were off, my dear sir; breach of promise trial—court is generally full in such cases. You had better ring for a coach, my dear sir, or we shall be rather late."

Mr. Pickwick immediately rang the bell; and a coach having been got, the four Pickwickians and Mr. Perker sat down inside, and drove to Guildhall, Sam Weller, and Perker's assistant, following in a cab.

"Put Mr. Pickwick's friends over there," said Perker to his assistant, when they reached the front hall of the court. "Mr. Pickwick himself had better sit by me. This way, my dear sir, this way." Taking Mr. Pickwick by the coat sleeve, the little man led him to the low seat just beneath the desks of the King's Counsel.

"That's the witness-box, I suppose?" said Mr. Pickwick, pointing to a kind of desk, with a brass rail, on his left hand.

"That's the witness-box, my dear sir," replied Perker, pulling out a quantity of papers from a blue bag which his assistant had just placed at his feet.

"And that," said Mr. Pickwick, pointing to a couple of enclosed seats on his right, "that's where the jurymen sit, is it not?"

"The very place, my dear sir," replied Perker.

Mr. Pickwick stood up in a state of great agitation, and took a glance at the court. There were already a fairly large number of spectators in the court, and numerous gentlemen in wigs, in the barristers' seats, who presented, as a body, all that pleasing and extensive variety of nose and whisker for which the Bar of England is so justly celebrated. The whole, to the great wonder of Mr. Pickwick, were divided into little groups who were talking and discussing the news of the day in the most unfeeling manner possible—just as if no trial at all were coming on.

Mr. Phunky, who had been retained to help Mr. Sergeant * Snubbin, Mr. Pickwick's counsel, bowed as he entered and attracted Mr. Pickwick's attention; and he had scarcely returned it, when Mr. Sergeant Snubbin appeared, and, after shaking hands with Perker, withdrew. Then there entered two or three more sergeants; and among them, one with a fat body and a red face, who nodded in a friendly manner to Mr. Sergeant Snubbin, and said it was a fine morning.

"Who's that red-faced man, who said it was a fine morning, and nodded to our counsel?" whispered Mr. Pickwick.

"Mr. Sergeant Buzfuz," replied Perker. "He's opposed to

* A title (now no longer used) for a barrister.

us; he leads on the other side. That gentleman behind him
is Mr. Skimpin, his junior."

Mr. Pickwick was on the point of inquiring how Mr.
Sergeant Buzfuz, who was counsel for the opposite party,
dared to tell Mr. Sergeant Snubbin, who was counsel for
him, that it was a fine morning, when he was interrupted by
a general rising of the barristers, and a loud cry of "Silence!"
from the officers of the court. Looking round, he found that
this was caused by the entrance of the judge.

Mr. Justice Stareleigh was a most particularly short man,
and so fat that he seemed all face and waistcoat. He rolled
in, upon two little bent legs, and having bowed gravely to
the Bar, who bowed gravely to him, put his little legs under-
neath his table, and his little three-cornered hat upon it;
and when Mr. Justice Stareleigh had done this, all you could
see of him was two queer little eyes, one broad pink face,
and somewhere about half of a big and very comical-looking
wig.

The judge had no sooner taken his seat than the officer on
the floor of the court called out "Silence!" in a commanding
voice, upon which another officer cried "Silence!" in an
angry manner, and three or four attendants shouted
"Silence!" in a voice of reproof.

At this moment a slight stir was noticeable in the body of
the court; and immediately afterwards Mrs. Bardell, supported by her friend Mrs. Cluppins, was led in, and placed,
in a state of collapse, at the other end of the seat on which
Mr. Pickwick sat. An extra-large umbrella was then handed
in by Mr. Dodson, and a pair of gloves by Mr. Fogg, each
of whom had prepared a most sympathising and sorrowful
face for the occasion. Master Bardell was then led in. At the
sight of her child, Mrs. Bardell started; suddenly remembering herself, she kissed him in a wild manner; then falling
back into a state of hysterical stupidity, the good lady re-
quested to be informed where she was. In reply to this, Mrs.
Cluppins turned her head away and wept, while Messrs.
Dodson and Fogg begged the plaintiff to calm herself. Sergeant Buzfuz rubbed his eyes very hard with a large white

handkerchief, and gave an appealing look towards the jury, while the judge was visibly affected, and several of the spectators tried to cough down their emotion.

"Very good notion that, indeed," whispered Perker to Mr. Pickwick. "Fine fellows those Dodson and Fogg; excellent ideas of effect, my dear sir, excellent."

As Perker spoke, Mrs. Bardell began to recover by slow degrees, while Mrs. Cluppins, after a careful examination of Master Bardell's clothes, placed him on the floor of the court in front of his mother—a commanding position in which he could not fail to awaken the full pity and sympathy of both judge and jury.

"Bardell and Pickwick," cried a gentleman in black, announcing the case, which stood first on the list.

"I am for the plaintiff, my Lord," said Mr. Sergeant Buzfuz.

"Who is with you, Brother Buzfuz?" said the judge. Mr. Skimpin bowed, to show that he was.

"I appear for the defendant, my Lord," said Mr. Sergeant Snubbin.

"Anybody with you, Brother Snubbin?" inquired the judge.

"Mr. Phunky, my Lord," replied Sergeant Snubbin.

"Sergeant Buzfuz and Mr. Skimpin for the plaintiff," said the judge, writing down the names in his note-book, and reading as he wrote; "for the defendant, Sergeant Snubbin and Mr. Monkey."

"Beg your Lordship's pardon, Phunky."

"Oh, very good," said the judge; "I never had the pleasure of hearing the gentleman's name before." Here Mr. Phunky bowed and smiled, and the judge bowed and smiled too, and then Mr. Phunky, blushing into the very whites of his eyes, tried to look as if he didn't know that everybody was gazing at him, a thing which no man ever succeeded in doing yet, or in all reasonable probability, ever will.

"Go on," said the judge.

The attendants again called silence, and Mr. Skimpin proceeded to "open the case" (and the case appeared to have very little inside it when he had opened it, for he kept such particulars as he knew completely to himself), and sat down, after an interval of three minutes, leaving the jury in precisely the same advanced stage of wisdom as they were in before.

Sergeant Buzfuz then rose with all the majesty and dignity which the serious nature of the proceedings demanded, and having whispered to Dodson and conferred briefly with Fogg, pulled his gown over his shoulders, settled his wig, and addressed the jury.

Sergeant Buzfuz began by saying that never, in the whole course of his professional experience—never, from the very first moment of his applying himself to the study and practice of the law—had he approached a case with feelings of such deep emotion, or with such a heavy sense of the responsibility imposed upon him—a responsibility, he would say, which he could never have supported, were he not strengthened by a conviction so strong, that it amounted to absolute certainty, that the cause of truth and justice, or, in other words, the cause of his much-injured and most unhappy client, must win the day with the high-minded and intelligent dozen of men whom he now saw in that box before him.

Counsel usually begin in this way, because it puts the jury on the very best terms with themselves, and makes them think what sharp fellows they must be. A visible effect was produced immediately, several jurymen beginning to take lengthy notes with the utmost eagerness.

"You have heard from my learned friend, gentlemen," continued Sergeant Buzfuz, well knowing that, from the learned friend referred to, the gentlemen of the jury had heard just nothing at all—"you have heard from my learned friend, gentlemen, that this is an action for a breach of promise of marriage, in which the damages are laid at £1,500. But you have not heard from my learned friend what are the facts and circumstances of the case. Those facts and circumstances, gentlemen, you shall hear described by me, and proved by the trustworthy female whom I will place in that box before you."

Here Mr. Sergeant Buzfuz, with a tremendous emphasis on the word "box," struck his table with a mighty sound, and glanced at Dodson and Fogg, who nodded admiration of the sergeant and indignant defiance of the defendant.

"The plaintiff, gentlemen," continued Sergeant Buzfuz in

Mr. Sergeant Buzfuz addresses the jury
(from the illustration by Phiz)

a soft and sorrowful voice, "the plaintiff is a widow; yes, gentlemen, a widow. The late Mr. Bardell, after enjoying for many years the admiration and confidence of his sovereign, as one of the guardians of his royal incomes, slipped almost unnoticed from the world, to look elsewhere for that rest and peace which a custom-house can never afford."

At this moving description of the death of Mr. Bardell, who had been knocked on the head with a quart-pot in a public-house cellar, the learned sergeant's voice trembled, and he proceeded, with emotion:

"Some time before his death he had stamped his likeness upon a little boy. With this little boy, the only memory of her lost customs-officer, Mrs. Bardell shrank from the world, and clung to the retirement and peace of Goswell Street; and here she placed in her front window a written notice, bearing this inscription—'Rooms furnished for a single gentleman. Inquire within.'" Here Sergeant Buzfuz paused, while several gentlemen of the jury took a note of the document.

"There is no date to that, is there?" inquired a juror.

"There is no date, gentlemen," replied Sergeant Buzfuz; "but I am instructed to say that it was put in the plaintiff's window just this time three years ago. I call the attention of the jury to the wording of this document—'Rooms furnished for a single gentleman'! Mrs. Bardell's opinions of the opposite sex, gentlemen, were formed from a long and deep study of the priceless qualities of her lost husband. She had no fear, she had no distrust, she had no suspicion; all was confidence and trust. 'Mr. Bardell,' said the widow; 'Mr. Bardell was a man of honour, Mr. Bardell was once a single gentleman himself; to single gentlemen I look for protection, for assistance, for comfort, and for consolation; in single gentlemen I shall continually see something to remind me of what Mr. Bardell was when he first won my young and untried affections; to a single gentleman, then, shall my lodgings be let.' Moved by this beautiful and touching impulse (among the best impulses of our imperfect nature, gentlemen), the lonely and desolate widow dried her tears, furnished her first floor, caught her innocent boy to her breast, and put the bill up in her window. Did it remain there long? No. The snake was on the watch, the trap was laid, the attack was being prepared, the schemer was at work. Before the bill had been in the window three days—three days, gentlemen—a being, erect upon two legs, and bearing all the outward appearance of a man, and not of a monster, knocked at the door of Mrs. Bardell's house. He inquired within—he took the lodgings; and on the very next day he entered into possession of them. This man was Pickwick—Pickwick, the defendant."

Sergeant Buzfuz, who had proceeded with such force that his face was a bright red, here paused for breath. The silence awoke Mr. Justice Stareleigh, who immediately wrote down something with a pen without any ink in it, and looked un-usually wise, to impress the jury with the belief that he always thought most deeply with his eyes shut. Sergeant Buzfuz proceeded:

"Of this man Pickwick I will say little; the subject presents but few attractions; and I, gentlemen, am not the man, nor are you, gentlemen, the men, to delight in the study of disgusting heartlessness and of systematic villainy."

Here Mr. Pickwick, who had been suffering in silence for some time, gave a violent start, as if some vague idea of attacking Sergeant Buzfuz, in the majestic presence of justice and law, suggested itself to his mind. A warning glance from Perker stopped him, and he listened to the learned gentleman's continuation with a look of indignation, which contrasted forcibly with the admiring face of Mrs. Cluppins.

Sergeant Buzfuz, having partially recovered from the high moral state into which he had worked himself, continued:

"I shall show you, gentlemen, that for two years Pickwick continued to live constantly, and without interruption, at Mrs. Bardell's house. I shall show you that Mrs. Bardell, during the whole of that time, waited on him, attended to his comforts, cooked his meals, looked out his linen for the washerwoman when it went away, mended, aired, and pre-pared it for wearing when it came home, and, in short, enjoyed his fullest trust and confidence. I shall show you that, on many occasions, he gave halfpence, and on some occasions even sixpences, to her little boy; and I shall prove to you, by a witness whose evidence it will be impossible for my learned friend to weaken or contradict, that on one occasion he patted the boy on the head and made use of this remarkable expression, 'How should you like to have another father?' I shall prove to you, gentlemen, that about a year ago, Pickwick suddenly began to stay away from home, during long intervals, as if with the intention of gradually breaking off from my client; but I shall show you also, that his resolution was not at that time sufficiently strong, or that his better feelings conquered, if better feelings he has, or that the charms and character of my client won the day against his unmanly intentions, by proving to you that, on one occasion, when he returned from the country, he distinctly and in terms offered her marriage: previously, however, taking special care that there would be no witness to their solemn contract; and I am in a situation to prove to you, on the evidence of three of his own friends—most unwilling witnesses, gentlemen—most unwilling witnesses—that on that morning he was discovered by them holding the plaintiff in his arms, and calming her agitation by his caresses and endearments.''

A visible impression was produced upon the whole court by this part of the learned sergeant's speech. Drawing out two very small scraps of paper, he proceeded:

"And now, gentlemen, but one word more. Two letters have passed between these parties, letters which are admitted to be in the handwriting of the defendant, and which speak indeed for themselves. The letters, too, show the character of the man. They are not open, passionate, expressive letters, breathing nothing but the language of affectionate attachment. They are artful, secretive, underhanded communications, but, fortunately, far more conclusive than if written in the most glowing language and the most poetic style—letters that must be viewed with a cautious and suspicious eye—letters that were evidently intended at the time, by Pickwick, to mislead and deceive any third parties into whose hands they might fall. Let me read the first: 'Garraway's, twelve o'clock. Dear Mrs. B.—Chops and tomato sauce. Yours, Pickwick.' Gentlemen, chops! Good heavens! And tomato sauce! Gentlemen, is the happiness of a sensitive and trusting female to be trifled away by such shallow tricks as these? The next has no date whatever, which is in itself suspicious. 'Dear Mrs. B., I shall not be at home till to-morrow. Slow coach.' And then follows this very remarkable expression. 'Don't trouble yourself about the warming-pan.' The warming-pan! Why, gentlemen, who does trouble himself about a warming-pan? When was the peace of mind of man or woman broken or disturbed by a warming-pan, which is in itself a harmless, a useful, and I will add, gentlemen, a comforting article of domestic furniture? Why is Mrs. Bardell so earnestly begged not to agitate herself about this warming-pan, unless (as is no doubt the case) it is a mere cover for hidden fire—a mere substitute previously agreed on for some endearing word or promise and artfully contrived by Pickwick with a view to the desertion he had already planned, and which I am not in a condition to explain? And what does this reference to the slow coach mean? For all I know, it may be a reference to Pickwick himself, who has most unquestionably been a criminally slow coach during the whole of this business, but whose speed will now be very unexpectedly increased, and whose wheels, gentlemen, as he will find to his cost, will very soon be greased by you!"

Mr. Sergeant Buzfuz paused in this place, to see whether the jury smiled at his joke; but as nobody saw it, the learned sergeant considered it advisable to return to his solemn manner before he concluded.

"But enough of this, gentlemen," said Mr. Sergeant Buzfuz, "it is difficult to smile with an aching heart; it is not right to joke when our deepest sympathies are awakened. My client's hopes and future are ruined, and it is no figure of speech to say that her occupation is gone indeed. The bill is down—but there is no lodger. Worthy single gentlemen pass and repass—but there is no invitation for them to inquire within or without. All is dark and silent in the house; even the voice of the child is lowered; his childish sports are disregarded when his mother weeps. But Pickwick, gentlemen, Pickwick, the heartless destroyer of this domestic oasis in the desert of Goswell Street—Pickwick, who comes before you to-day with his heartless tomato sauce and warming-pans—Pickwick still rears his head with unblushing boldness, and gazes without a sigh on the ruin he has made. Damages, gentlemen—heavy damages is the only punishment which you can give him; the only consolation you can grant to my client. And for those damages she now appeals to an enlightened, a high-minded, a right-feeling, a conscientious, a dispassionate, a sympathising, a thoughtful jury of her civilised countrymen."

On this beautiful climax, Mr. Sergeant Buzfuz sat down, and Mr. Justice Stareleigh woke up.

"Call Elizabeth Cluppins," said Sergeant Buzfuz, rising a minute afterwards with renewed vigour.

The nearest attendant called for Elizabeth Tuppins; another one, at a little distance off, demanded Elizabeth Jupkins; and a third rushed in a breathless state into King Street, and screamed for Elizabeth Muffins till he was hoarse.

Meanwhile Mrs. Cluppins, with the combined assistance of Mrs. Bardell, Mr. Dodson, and Mr. Fogg, was pushed into the witness-box; and when she was safely seated on the top step, Mrs. Bardell stood on the bottom one, with the pocket-handkerchief and gloves in one hand, and a glass bottle that might hold about a quarter of a pint of smelling-salts in the other, ready for any emergency.

"Mrs. Cluppins," said Sergeant Buzfuz, "please calm yourself, madam." Of course, directly Mrs. Cluppins was desired to calm herself, she sobbed with increased violence, and gave several alarming signs of an approaching fainting fit, or, as she afterwards said, of her feelings being too much for her.

"Do you remember, Mrs. Cluppins," said Sergeant Buzfuz after a few unimportant questions—"do you remember being in Mrs. Bardell's back stairs, on one particular morning last July, when she was dusting Pickwick's room?"

"Yes, my Lord and jury, I do," replied Mrs. Cluppins.

"Mr. Pickwick's sitting-room was the first-floor in the front, I believe?"

"Yes, it was, sir," replied Mrs. Cluppins.

"What were you doing in the back room, madam?" inquired the little judge.

"My Lord and jury," said Mrs. Cluppins, with increasing agitation, "I will not deceive you."

"You had better not, madam," said the little judge. .

"I was there," continued Mrs. Cluppins, "unknown to Mrs. Bardell; I had been out with a little basket, gentlemen, to buy three pound of new potatoes, which were three pound twopence halfpenny, when I saw Mrs. Bardell's street door partly open. I walked in, gentlemen, just to say good morning, and went, in an innocent manner, upstairs and into the back room. Gentlemen, there was the sound of voices in the front room and——"

"And you listened, I believe, Mrs. Cluppins?" said Sergeant Buzfuz.

"Begging your pardon, sir," replied Mrs. Cluppins in a majestic manner, "I would scorn the action. The voices were very loud, sir, and forced themselves upon my ear."

"Well, Mrs. Cluppins, you were not listening, but you heard the voices. Was one of those voices Pickwick's?"

"Yes, it was, sir."

And Mrs. Cluppins, after distinctly stating that Mr. Pickwick was speaking to Mrs. Bardell, repeated by slow degrees, and after many questions, the conversation with which our readers are already familiar.

The jury looked suspicious, and Mr. Sergeant Buzfuz smiled and sat down. They looked positively awful when Sergeant Snubbin said he would not cross-examine the witness, for Mr. Pickwick wished it to be distinctly stated that her story was in substance correct.

Mrs. Cluppins, having once broken the ice, thought it a favourable opportunity for entering into a short account of her own domestic affairs; but the little judge interrupted in a most bad-tempered manner; and the effect of the interruption was that the worthy lady was politely taken out of court without further delay.

"Nathaniel Winkle!" said Mr. Skimpin.

"Here!" replied a feeble voice. Mr. Winkle entered the witness-box, and having been sworn, bowed to the judge with considerable respect.

"Don't look at me, sir," said the judge sharply, in reply to the bow; "look at the jury."

Mr. Winkle obeyed the instruction, and looked at the place where he thought it most probable the jury might be; for seeing anything in his present state of mental confusion was wholly out of the question.

Mr. Winkle was then examined by Mr. Skimpin, who, being a promising young man of two or three and forty, was of course anxious to confuse a witness who was notoriously in favour of the other side, as much as he could.

"Now, sir," said Mr. Skimpin, "have the goodness to let his Lordship and the jury know what your name is, will you?" and Mr. Skimpin put his head on one side to listen with great sharpness to the answer, and glanced at the jury meanwhile, as if to imply that he rather expected Mr. Winkle's natural habit of lying would lead him into giving some name which did not belong to him.

"Winkle," replied the witness.

"What's your Christian name, sir?" angrily inquired the little judge.

"Nathaniel, sir."

"Daniel—any other name?"

"Nathaniel, sir—my Lord, I mean."

"Nathaniel Daniel, or Daniel Nathaniel?"

"No, my Lord, only Nathaniel; not Daniel at all."

"What did you tell me it was Daniel for, then, sir?" inquired the judge.

"I didn't, my Lord," replied Mr. Winkle.

"You did, sir," replied the judge with a severe frown. "How could I have got Daniel on my notes, unless you told me so, sir?"

This argument was, of course, unanswerable.

"Mr. Winkle has rather a short memory, my Lord," said Mr. Skimpin with another glance at the jury. "We shall find means to refresh it before we have quite done with him, I dare say."

"You had better be careful, sir," said the little judge, with an angry look at the witness.

Poor Mr. Winkle bowed and tried to put on an easiness of manner which gave him rather the air of a pickpocket caught in the act.

"Now, Mr. Winkle," said Mr. Skimpin, "attend to me, if you please, sir; and let me recommend you, for your own sake, to bear in mind his Lordship's instructions to be careful. I believe you are a particular friend of Mr. Pickwick, the defendant, are you not?"

"I have known Mr. Pickwick now, as well as I remember at this moment, nearly——"

"Please, Mr. Winkle, do not try to avoid the question. Are you, or are you not, a particular friend of the defendant's?"

"I was just about to say that——"

"Will you, or will you not, answer my question, sir?"

"If you don't answer the question, you'll be punished, sir," interrupted the little judge, looking over his note-book.

"Come, sir," said Mr. Skimpin, "yes or no, if you please."

"Yes, I am," replied Mr. Winkle.

"Yes, you are. And why couldn't you say that at once, sir? Perhaps you know the plaintiff, too? Eh, Mr. Winkle?"

"I don't know her; I've seen her."

"Oh, you don't know her, but you've seen her? Now, have the goodness to tell the gentlemen of the jury what you mean by that, Mr. Winkle?"

"I mean that I am not familiar with her, but I have seen her when I went to call on Mr. Pickwick, in Goswell Street."

"How often have you seen her, sir?"

"How often?"

"Yes, Mr. Winkle, how often? I'll repeat the question for you a dozen times, if you wish it, sir." And the learned gentleman, with a firm and steady frown, placed his hands on his hips, and smiled suspiciously to the jury.

On this question there began the cross-examination customary on such points. First of all, Mr. Winkle said it was quite impossible for him to say how many times he had seen Mrs. Bardell. Then he was asked if he had seen her twenty times, to which he replied, "Certainly—more than that." Then he was asked whether he hadn't seen her a hundred times—whether he couldn't swear that he had seen her more than fifty times—whether he didn't know that he had seen her at least seventy-five times, and so on; the satisfactory conclusion which was arrived at at last being that he had better take care and mind what he was saying. The witness having been by these means reduced to a state of nervous confusion, the examination was continued as follows:

"Now, Mr. Winkle, do you remember calling on the defendant Pickwick at these rooms in the plaintiff's house in Goswell Street, on one particular morning, in the month of July last?"

"Yes, I do."

"Were you accompanied on that occasion by a friend of the name of Tupman, and another by the name of Snodgrass?"

"Yes, I was."

"Are they here?"

"Yes, they are," replied Mr. Winkle, looking very earnestly towards the spot where his friends were sitting.

"Please attend to me, Mr. Winkle, and never mind your friends," said Mr. Skimpin, with another expressive look at the jury. "They must tell their stories without any previous consultation with you, if none has yet taken place" (another look at the jury). "Now, sir, tell the gentlemen of the jury what you saw on entering the defendant's room on this particular morning. Come; out with it, sir; we must have it, sooner or later."

"The defendant, Mr. Pickwick, was holding the plaintiff with his arms round her waist," replied Mr. Winkle with natural hesitation, "and the plaintiff appeared to have fainted away."

"Did you hear the defendant say anything?"

"I heard him call Mrs. Bardell a good woman, and I heard him ask her to calm herself, for what a situation it was, if anybody should come, or words to that effect."

"Now, Mr. Winkle, I have only one more question to ask you, and I beg you to bear in mind his Lordship's warning. Will you swear that Pickwick, the defendant, did not say on the occasion in question: 'My dear Mrs. Bardell, you're a good woman; calm yourself to this situation, for to this situation you must come,' or words to that effect?"

"I—I didn't understand him so, certainly," said Mr. Winkle, astounded at this clever rearrangement of the few words he had heard. "I was on the stairs, and couldn't hear distinctly; the impression on my mind is——"

"The gentlemen of the jury want none of the impressions on your mind, Mr. Winkle, which I fear would be of little service to honest, straightforward men," interrupted Mr. Skimpin. "You were on the stairs, and didn't distinctly hear; but you will not swear that Pickwick did not make use of the expressions I have quoted? Do I understand that?"

"No, I will not," replied Mr. Winkle; and down sat Mr. Skimpin with a triumphant expression.

Mr. Pickwick's case had not gone off in so particularly happy a manner, up to this point, that it could very well afford to have any additional suspicion thrown upon it. But as it could afford to be placed in a rather better light, if possible, Mr. Phunky rose for the purpose of getting something important out of Mr. Winkle in cross-examination. Whether he did get anything important out of him will immediately appear.

"I believe, Mr. Winkle," said Mr. Phunky, "that Mr. Pickwick is not a young man?"

"Oh no," replied Mr. Winkle; "old enough to be my father."

"You have told my learned friend that you have known Mr. Pickwick a long time. Had you ever any reason to suppose or believe that he was about to be married?"

"Oh no; certainly not," replied Mr. Winkle with so much

eagerness that Mr. Phunky ought to have got him out of the box with all possible haste. Lawyers agree that there are two kinds of particularly bad witnesses—an unwilling witness, and a too-willing witness; it was Mr. Winkle's fate to figure in both characters.

"I will even go further than this, Mr. Winkle," continued Mr. Phunky, in a most smooth and confident manner. "Did you ever see anything in Mr. Pickwick's manner and conduct towards the opposite sex, to lead you to believe that he ever thought of matrimony these last few years, in any case?"

"Oh no; certainly not," replied Mr. Winkle.

"Has his behaviour, when females have been in the case, always been that of a man who, having reached a pretty advanced period of life, content with his own occupations and amusements, treats them only as a father might his daughters?"

"Not the least doubt of it," replied Mr. Winkle, in the fullness of his heart. "That is—yes—oh, yes—certainly."

"You have never known anything in his behaviour towards Mrs. Bardell, or any other female, in the least degree suspicious?" said Mr. Phunky, preparing to sit down; for Sergeant Snubbin was winking at him.

"No—n—no," replied Mr. Winkle, "except on one trifling occasion, which, I have no doubt, might be easily explained."

Now, if the unfortunate Mr. Phunky had sat down when Sergeant Snubbin had winked at him, or if Sergeant Buzfuz had stopped this unusual cross-examination at the beginning (which he knew better than to do; observing Mr. Winkle's anxiety, and well knowing it would, in all probability, lead to something useful to him), this unfortunate admission would not have slipped out. The moment the words fell from Mr. Winkle's lips, Mr. Phunky sat down, and Sergeant Snubbin rather hastily told him he might leave the box, which Mr. Winkle prepared to do with great readiness, when Sergeant Buzfuz stopped him.

"Stay, Mr. Winkle, stay!" said Sergeant Buzfuz. "Will your Lordship have the goodness to ask him what this one instance of suspicious behaviour towards females on the part

44

of this gentleman, who is old enough to be his father, was?"

"You hear what the learned counsel says, sir," remarked the judge, turning to the miserable and agonised Mr. Winkle. "Describe the occasion to which you refer."

"My Lord," said Mr. Winkle, trembling with anxiety, "I —I'd rather not."

"Perhaps so," said the little judge; "but you must."

In the deep silence of the whole court, Mr. Winkle stammered out that the trifling circumstance of suspicion was Mr. Pickwick's being found in a lady's bedroom at midnight; which had resulted, he believed, in the breaking off of the proposed marriage of the lady in question, and had led, he knew, to the whole party being forcibly carried before the magistrate and justice of the peace for the town of Ipswich!

"You may leave the box, sir," said Sergeant Snubbin. Mr. Winkle did leave the box, and rushed with feverish haste to the George and Vulture, where he was discovered some hours after, by the waiter, groaning in a hollow and miserable manner, with his head buried beneath the sofa cushions.

Tracy Tupman and Augustus Snodgrass were called in turn into the box; both confirmed the evidence of their unhappy friend; and each was driven almost to desperation by excessive questioning.

Sergeant Buzfuz now rose with more importance than he had yet exhibited, if that were possible, and shouted: "Call Samuel Weller."

It was quite unnecessary to call Samuel Weller, for Samuel Weller stepped quickly into the box the moment his name was called, and placing his hat on the floor, and his arms on the rail, took a bird's-eye view of the Bar, and a thorough examination of the Judge with a remarkably cheerful and lively aspect.

"What's your name, sir?" inquired the judge.

"Sam Weller, my Lord," replied that gentleman, and bowing his respects, turned, with perfect cheerfulness towards Sergeant Buzfuz.

"Now, Mr. Weller," said Sergeant Buzfuz.

"Now, sir," replied Sam.

"I believe you are in the service of Mr. Pickwick, the defendant in this case? Speak up, if you please, Mr. Weller."

"I mean to speak up, sir," replied Sam. "I am in the service of that gentleman, and a very good service it is."

"Little to do, and plenty to get, I suppose?" said Sergeant Buzfuz humorously.

"Oh, quite enough to get, sir, as the soldier said when they ordered him three hundred and fifty strokes of the whip," replied Sam.

"You must not tell us what the soldier, or any other man, said, sir," interrupted the judge; "it's not evidence."

"Very good, my Lord," replied Sam.

"Do you remember anything particular happening on the morning when you were first engaged by the defendant; eh, Mr. Weller?" said Sergeant Buzfuz.

"Yes, I do, sir," replied Sam.

"Have the goodness to tell the jury what it was."

"I had a regular new set of clothes that morning, gentlemen of the jury," said Sam, "and that was a very particular and uncommon circumstance with me in those days."

At this point there was a general laugh; and the little judge, looking with an angry expression over his desk, said, "You had better be careful, sir."

"So Mr. Pickwick said at the time, my Lord," replied Sam, "and I was very careful of that suit of clothes; very careful indeed, my Lord."

The judge looked sternly at Sam for fully two minutes, but Sam's face was so perfectly calm and innocent that the judge said nothing, and instructed Sergeant Buzfuz to proceed.

"Do you mean to tell me, Mr. Weller," said Sergeant Buzfuz, folding his arms emphatically, and turning half-round to the jury, as if silently promising that he would upset the witness yet—"do you mean to tell me, Mr. Weller, that you saw nothing of this fainting on the part of the plaintiff in the arms of the defendant, which you have heard described by the witnesses?"

"Certainly not," replied Sam; "I was just outside till they

46

called me up, and then the old lady was not there."

"Now, listen, Mr. Weller," said Sergeant Buzfuz, dipping a large pen into the inkstand before him, for the purpose of frightening Sam with a pretence of taking down his answer. "You were just outside, and yet saw nothing of what was happening. Have you a pair of eyes, Mr. Weller?"

"Yes, I have a pair of eyes," replied Sam, "and that's just it. If they were a pair of patent double million magnifying glasses of extra power, perhaps I might be able to see through a flight of stairs and a wooden door; but being only eyes, you see, my sight's limited."

At this answer, which was given without the slightest appearance of irritation, and with the most complete simplicity and calmness of manner, the spectators laughed, the little judge smiled, and Sergeant Buzfuz looked particularly foolish. After a short consultation with Dodson & Fogg, the learned sergeant again turned towards Sam, and said, with a painful effort to hide his annoyance, "Now, Mr. Weller, I'll ask you a question on another point, if you please."

"If you please, sir," replied Sam, with the utmost good-humour.

"Do you remember going up to Mrs. Bardell's house, one night in November last?"

"Oh yes; very well."

"Oh, you do remember that, Mr. Weller," said Sergeant Buzfuz, recovering his spirits; "I thought we should get at something at last."

"I rather thought that, too, sir," replied Sam; and at this the spectators laughed again.

"Well! I suppose you went up to have a little talk about this trial—eh, Mr. Weller?" said Sergeant Buzfuz, looking knowingly at the jury.

"I went up to pay the rent; but we did get to talking about the trial," replied Sam.

"Oh, you did get to talking about the trial," said Sergeant Buzfuz, brightening up with the expectation of some important discovery. "Now, what passed about the trial; will you have the goodness to tell us, Mr. Weller?"

47

"With all the pleasure in the world, sir," replied Sam. "After a few unimportant remarks from the two worthy females here to-day, the ladies got into a very great state of admiration at the honourable conduct of Mr. Dodson and Mr. Fogg—those two gentlemen sitting near you now." This, of course, drew general attention to Dodson and Fogg, who tried to look as noble as possible.

"The lawyers for the plaintiff," said Mr. Sergeant Buzfuz. "Well! They spoke in high praise of the honourable conduct of Messrs. Dodson and Fogg, the lawyers for the plaintiff, did they?"

"Yes," said Sam; "they said what a very generous thing it was of them to have taken up the case on spec,* and to charge nothing at all for costs, unless they got them out of Mr. Pickwick."

At this very unexpected reply, the spectators laughed again, and Dodson and Fogg, turning very red, leaned over to Sergeant Buzfuz, and in a hurried manner whispered something in his ear.

"You are quite right," said Sergeant Buzfuz out loud, with pretended calmness. "It's perfectly useless, my Lord, attempting to get at any evidence through the utter stupidity of this witness. I will not trouble the court by asking him any more questions. Stand down, sir."

"Would any other gentleman like to ask me anything?" inquired Sam, taking up his hat and looking round the court.

"Not I, Mr. Weller, thank you," said Sergeant Snubbin, laughing.

"You may get down, sir," said Sergeant Buzfuz, waving his hand impatiently. Sam went down accordingly, after doing Messrs. Dodson & Fogg's case as much harm as he conveniently could, and saying just as little about Mr. Pickwick as possible, which was precisely the object he had had in view all along.

"I have no objection to admit, my Lord," said Sergeant

* On spec = on speculation, i.e. taking the risk on the chance of a successful result (*slang*).

48

Snubbin, "if it will save the examination of another witness, that Mr. Pickwick has retired from business, and is a gentleman of considerable independent property."

"Very well," said Sergeant Buzfuz, putting in the two letters to be read; "then that's my case, my Lord."

Sergeant Snubbin then addressed the jury for the defendant; and a very long and a very emphatic address he gave, in which he spoke the highest possible praises of the conduct and character of Mr. Pickwick; but as our readers are far better able to form a correct judgment of that gentleman's qualities than Sergeant Snubbin could possibly be, we do not feel it necessary to enter at any length into the learned gentleman's remarks. He attempted to show that the letters which had been exhibited merely related to Mr. Pickwick's dinner, or to the preparations for receiving him in his rooms on his return from some country visit. It is sufficient to add in general terms, that he did the best he could for Mr. Pickwick; and the best, as everybody knows, is all· that anyone can do.

Mr. Justice Stareleigh summed up, in the old-established and most approved manner. He read as much of his notes to the jury as he could make out at so short a notice, and made running comments on the evidence as he went along. If Mrs. Bardell were right, it was perfectly clear that Mr. Pickwick was wrong, and if they thought the evidence of Mrs. Cluppins worthy of belief they would believe it, and, if they didn't, why, they wouldn't. If they were satisfied that a breach of promise of marriage had been committed, they would give their verdict in favour of the plaintiff·with such damages as they thought proper; and if, on the other hand, it appeared to them that no promise of marriage had ever been given, they would give their verdict in favour of the defendant with no damages at all. The jury then retired to their private room to talk the matter over, and the judge retired to his private room to refresh himself with a mutton-chop and a glass of sherry.

An anxious quarter of an hour passed; the jury came back; the judge was called in. Mr. Pickwick put on his glasses, and gazed at the foreman with an agitated face and a quickly beating heart.

"Gentlemen," said the individual in black, "are you all agreed upon your verdict?"

"We are," replied the foreman.

"Do you give your verdict in favour of the plaintiff, gentlemen, or in favour of the defendant?"

"The plaintiff."

"With what damages, gentlemen?"

"Seven hundred and fifty pounds."

Mr. Pickwick took off his glasses, carefully wiped them, folded them into their case, and put them in his pocket; then, having drawn on his gloves with great care, and stared at the foreman all the while, he mechanically followed Mr. Perker out of court.

They stopped in a side room while Perker paid the court charges, and here Mr. Pickwick was joined by his friends. Here, too, he met Messrs. Dodson & Fogg, rubbing their hands with every sign of outward satisfaction.

"Well, gentlemen," said Mr. Pickwick.

"Well, sir," said Dodson, for himself and partner.

"You imagine you'll get your costs, don't you, gentlemen?" said Mr. Pickwick.

Fogg said they thought it rather probable. Dodson smiled, and said they'd try.

"You may try, and try again, Messrs. Dodson and Fogg," said Mr. Pickwick emphatically; "but not one farthing of costs or damages do you get from me, if I spend the rest of my existence in a debtor's prison."

"Ha, ha!" laughed Dodson. "You'll think better of that, before long, Mr. Pickwick."

"He, he, he! We'll soon see about that, Mr. Pickwick," grinned Fogg.

Speechless with indignation, Mr. Pickwick allowed himself to be led by his lawyer and friends to the door, and there assisted into a coach, which had been called for the purpose, by the ever-watchful Sam Weller.

OLIVER TWIST MEETS FAGIN
(from *Oliver Twist*)

[Oliver, who has lost his home and parents, suffers many cruelties at school and as an apprentice. He determines to escape, and walks to London to make his fortune.]

EARLY on the seventh morning after he had left his native place, Oliver limped slowly into the little town of Barnet. The windows were closed; the street was empty; no one was yet awake. The sun was rising in all its glorious beauty; but the light only served to show the boy his own loneliness and desolation, as he sat, with bleeding feet and covered with dust, upon a doorstep.

By degrees, the windows were opened; the curtains were drawn back, and people began passing to and fro. Some few stopped to gaze at Oliver for a moment or two, or turned round to stare at him as they hurried past; but no one helped him, or troubled themselves to inquire how he came there. He had no heart to beg. And there he sat.

He had been crouching on the step for some time, gazing listlessly at the coaches as they passed through, when he was roused by observing that a boy, who had passed him carelessly some minutes before, had returned, and was now looking at him most earnestly from the opposite side of the way. He took little notice of this at first; but the boy remained in the same position of close observation so long, that Oliver raised his head, and returned his steady look. Upon this, the boy crossed over: and walking close up to Oliver, said,

"Hullo, young fellow! What's the row?"

The boy who addressed this inquiry to the young traveller was about his own age: but one of the queerest-looking boys that Oliver had ever seen. He had a small nose, narrow forehead and a common face; and was as dirty a youth as one would wish to see: but he had about him all the ways and manners of a man. He was short for his age: with rather bow-legs, and little, sharp, ugly eyes. His hat was placed on the top of his head so lightly, that it threatened to fall off every moment—and would have done so, very often, if the wearer had not had a habit of every now and then giving his head a sudden twist, which brought it back to its old place again. He wore a man's coat which reached nearly to his heels. He had rolled the sleeves back, half-way up his arm, to get his hands out: apparently with the intention of pushing them into the pockets of his trousers; for there he kept them. He was, altogether, as self-confident a young gentleman as ever stood four feet six inches, or something less, in his boots.

"Hullo, young fellow! What's the row?" said this strange young gentleman to Oliver.

"I am very hungry and tired," replied Oliver, the tears standing in his eyes as he spoke. "I have walked a long way. I have been walking these last seven days."

"Walking for seven days!" said the young gentleman. "Oh, I see. Beak's order, eh? But," he added, noticing Oliver's look of surprise, "I suppose you don't know what a beak is, my fine companion."

Oliver mildly replied that he had always heard a bird's mouth described by the term in question.

"My eyes! How green*!" exclaimed the young gentleman. "Why, a beak's a magistrate; and when you walk by a beak's order, it's not straightforward, but always going up, and never coming down again.

"Going to London?" continued the strange boy.

"Yes."

"Got any lodgings?"

"No."

"Money?"

"No."

The strange boy whistled, and put his arms into his pockets as far as his big coat sleeves would let them go.

"Do you live in London?" inquired Oliver.

"Yes, I do, when I'm at home," replied the boy. "I sup-

* Green = simple-minded.

pose you want some place to sleep in to-night, don't you?"

"I do indeed," answered Oliver. "I have not slept under a roof since I left the country."

"Don't worry yourself about that," said the young gentleman. "I've got to be in London to-night; and I know a respectable old gentleman who lives there, who'll give you lodgings for nothing, and never ask for the change—that is, if any gentleman he knows introduces you. And doesn't he know me? Oh no! Not in the least! By no means. Certainly not!"

The young gentleman smiled, as if to show that the last few words were playfully ironical.

This unexpected offer of shelter was too tempting to be resisted; especially as it was immediately followed by the promise that the old gentleman referred to would doubtless provide Oliver with a comfortable job, without loss of time. This led to a more friendly and confidential dialogue; from which Oliver discovered that his friend's name was Jack Dawkins, better known to his friends as the "Artful Dodger"; and that he was a special pet and pupil of the old gentleman before mentioned.

As Jack Dawkins objected to their entering London before night, it was nearly eleven o'clock when they reached the gate at Islington.

Passing through numerous streets, they came into Saffron Hill the Great; along which the Dodger hurried at a great speed, directing Oliver to follow close at his heels.

Although Oliver had enough to occupy his attention in keeping sight of his leader, he could not help throwing a few hasty glances on either side of the road, as he passed along. A dirtier or more wretched place he had never seen. The street was very narrow and muddy, and the air was filled with horrible smells. There were a good many small shops; but the only thing in stock appeared to be crowds of children, who, even at that time of night, were crawling in and out of the doors, or screaming from the inside. The only places that seemed to prosper in the general poverty of the place were the public-houses; and in them, the lowest kinds of people were quarrelling with all their might. Covered ways and yards, which here and there branched off from the main street, revealed little knots of houses, where drunken men and women were lying in the dirt; and from several of the doorways, great ill-looking fellows were cautiously coming out, intent, to all appearance, on no very honest or harmless business.

Oliver was just considering whether he hadn't better run away, when they reached the bottom of the hill. His guide, catching him by the arm, pushed open the door of a house near Field Lane; and drawing him inside, closed it behind them.

"Now, then!" cried a voice from below, in reply to a whistle from the Dodger.

"Plummy and slam!" was the reply.

This seemed to be some watchword or signal that all was right; for the light of a feeble candle shone on the wall at the far end of the passage; and a man's face looked out from where a rail of the old kitchen staircase had broken away.

"There's two of you," said the man, pushing the candle farther out, and shading his eyes with his hand. "Who's the other one?"

"A new friend," replied Jack Dawkins, pulling Oliver forward.

"Where did he come from?"

"Greenland. Is Fagin upstairs?"

"Yes, he's sorting the wipes.* Up with you!" The candle was drawn back, and the face disappeared.

Oliver, feeling his way with one hand, and having the other firmly held by his companion, climbed with much difficulty the dark and broken stairs: which his guide went up with an ease and speed which showed he was very familiar with them. He threw open the door of a back-room, and drew Oliver in after him.

The walls and ceiling of the room were perfectly black with age and dirt. There was a rough wooden table before the fire: upon which were a candle, stuck in a ginger-beer

* Wipes = handkerchiefs (thieves' slang).

bottle, two or three pots, a loaf and butter, and a plate. In a
frying-pan, which was on the fire, and which was fastened to
the mantelpiece by a string, some sausages were cooking; and
standing over them, with a toasting-fork in his hand, was a
very old man whose villainous-looking and horrible face was

George Cruikshank

Oliver meets Fagin and the boys
(from the illustration by Cruikshank)

55

hidden by a quantity of coarse red hair. He was dressed in a greasy flannel gown, with his throat bare; and seemed to be dividing his attention between the frying-pan and a clothes-rail, over which a great number of silk handkerchiefs were hanging. Several rough beds made of old sacks were crowded together side by side on the floor. Seated round the table were four or five boys, none older than the Dodger, smoking long clay pipes, and drinking spirits with the air of middle-aged men. These all crowded about their companion as he whispered a few words to the old man; and then turned round and grinned at Oliver. So did the old man himself, toasting-fork in hand.

"This is him, Fagin," said Jack Dawkins; "my friend Oliver Twist." Fagin grinned; and, making a low bow to Oliver, took him by the hand, and hoped he should have the honour of knowing him well. Upon this, the young gentlemen with the pipes came round him, and shook both his hands very hard—especially the one in which he held his little bundle. One young gentleman was very anxious to hang up his cap for him; and another was so obliging as to put his hands in his pockets, in order that, as he was very tired, he might not have the trouble of emptying them, himself, when he went to bed. These attentions would probably have gone on much farther, but for a free exercise of Fagin's toasting-fork on the heads and shoulders of the affectionate youths who offered them.

"We are very glad to see you, Oliver, very," said Fagin. "Dodger, take off the sausages; and draw a seat near the fire for Oliver. Ah, you're staring at the pocket-handkerchiefs! eh, my dear! There are a good many of them, aren't there? We've just looked 'em out, ready for the wash; that's all, Oliver; that's all. Ha! ha! ha!"

The latter part of this speech was greeted by a noisy shout from all the hopeful pupils of the merry old gentleman. In the midst of which, they went to supper.

Oliver ate his share, and Fagin then mixed him a glass of hot gin and water; telling him to drink it quickly, because another gentleman wanted the glass. Oliver did as he was told. Immediately afterwards he felt himself gently lifted on to one of the sacks; and then he sank into a deep sleep.

It was late next morning when Oliver awoke, from a sound, long sleep. There was no other person in the room but old Fagin, who was boiling some coffee in a saucepan for breakfast, and whistling softly to himself as he stirred it round and round with an iron spoon. He would stop every now and then to listen when there was the slightest noise below: and when he had satisfied himself he would go on, whistling and stirring again, as before.

Oliver was not fully awake and saw Fagin through his half-closed eyes; heard his low whistling; and recognised the sound of the spoon scraping against the saucepan's sides.

When the coffee was done, Fagin took the saucepan off the fire. Standing, then, in an irresolute position for a few minutes, as if he did not know what to do, he turned round and looked at Oliver, and called him by his name. He did not answer, and was to all appearance asleep.

After satisfying himself on this point, Fagin stepped gently to the door: which he locked. He then drew out, as it seemed to Oliver, from some hole in the floor, a small box, which he placed carefully on the table. His eyes glistened as he raised the lid and looked in. Dragging an old chair to the table, he sat down; and took from it a magnificent gold watch, shining with jewels.

"Aha!" said Fagin, distorting his face with a horrible grin. "Clever dogs! Clever dogs! Faithful to the last! Never told the old parson where they were. Never peached * upon old Fagin! And why should they? It wouldn't have loosened the knot, or kept them from being hanged, a minute longer. No, no, no! Fine fellows! Fine fellows!"

With these, and other muttered remarks of a similar nature, Fagin once more put the watch in its place of safety. At least half a dozen more were in turn drawn out of the same box, and examined with equal pleasure; besides rings, brooches, bracelets, and other articles of jewellery of such

* To peach upon = inform on; betray (thieves' slang).

magnificent materials and costly workmanship, that Oliver had no idea, even, of their names.

Having replaced these treasures, Fagin took out another; so small that it lay in the palm of his hand. There seemed to be some sort of inscription on it; for Fagin laid it flat upon the table, and, shading it with his hand, gazed at it, long and earnestly. At length he put it down, as if despairing of success; and, leaning back in his chair, muttered:

"What a fine thing capital punishment is! Dead men never repent; dead men never bring awkward stories to light. Ah, it's a fine thing for the trade! Five of them hanging in a row, and none left to share the treasure or turn cowardly!"

As Fagin spoke these words, his bright dark eyes, which had been staring absent-mindedly before him, fell on Oliver's face; the boy's eyes were fixed on his in silent curiosity; and although the recognition was only for a moment—for the briefest space of time that can possibly be imagined—it was enough to show the old man that he had been observed. He closed the lid of the box with a loud crash; and, laying his hand on a bread-knife which was on the table, jumped up furiously. He trembled very much though; for, even in his terror, Oliver could see that the knife shook in the air.

"What's that?" said Fagin. "What do you watch me for? Why are you awake? What have you seen? Speak out, boy! Quick—quick! for your life!"

"I wasn't able to sleep any longer, sir," replied Oliver, timidly. "I am very sorry if I have disturbed you, sir."

"You were not awake an hour ago?" said Fagin, frowning fiercely at the boy.

"No! No, indeed!" replied Oliver.

"Are you sure?" cried Fagin, with a still fiercer look than before.

"Upon my word I was not, sir," replied Oliver, earnestly. "I was not, indeed, sir."

"That's all right, my dear," said Fagin, quickly returning to his old manner, and playing with the knife a little before he laid it down; pretending that he had picked it up in mere fun. "Of course I know that, my dear. I only tried to frighten you. You're a brave boy. Ha! ha! You're a brave boy, Oliver!" Fagin rubbed his hands with a grin, but glanced uneasily at the box, nevertheless.

"Did you see any of these pretty things, my dear?" said Fagin, laying his hand upon it after a short pause.

"Yes, sir," replied Oliver.

"Ah!" said Fagin, turning rather pale. "They—they're mine, Oliver; my little property. All I have to live on, in my old age. People call me a miser, my dear. Only a miser; that's all."

Oliver thought the old gentleman must be a decided miser to live in such a dirty place, with so many watches; but, thinking that perhaps his fondness for the Dodger and the other boys cost him a good deal of money, he only gave Fagin a respectful look, and asked if he might get up.

"Certainly, my dear, certainly," replied the old gentleman. "Stay. There's a jug of water in the corner by the door. Bring it here; and I'll give you a basin to wash in, my dear."

Oliver got up; walked across the room; and stooped for a moment to raise the jug. When he turned his head, the box was gone.

He had scarcely washed himself, and made everything tidy, by emptying the basin out of the window, as Fagin had told him, when the Dodger returned, accompanied by a very lively young friend, whom Oliver had seen smoking on the previous night, and who was now formally introduced to him as Charley Bates. The four sat down to breakfast on the coffee and some hot rolls and ham which the Dodger had brought home in his hat.

"Well," said Fagin, glancing artfully at Oliver and speaking to the Dodger, "I hope you've been at work this morning, my dears?"

"Hard," replied the Dodger.

"As nails," added Charles Bates.

"Good boys, good boys!" said Fagin. "What have you got, Dodger?"

"A couple of pocket-books," replied that young gentleman.

"Lined?" inquired Fagin, with eagerness.

"Pretty well," replied the Dodger, producing two pocket-books; one green and the other red.

"Not so heavy as they might be," said Fagin, after looking at the insides carefully; "but very neat and nicely made. Clever workman, isn't he, Oliver?"

"Very, indeed, sir," said Oliver. At which Mr. Charles Bates laughed loudly; very much to the astonishment of Oliver, who saw nothing to laugh at in anything that had happened.

"And what have you got, my dear?" said Fagin to Charley Bates.

"Wipes," replied Master Bates, at the same time producing four pocket-handkerchiefs.

"Well," said Fagin, examining them closely, "they're very good ones, very. You haven't marked them well, though, Charley; so the marks shall be picked out with a needle, and we'll teach Oliver how to do it. Shall we, Oliver, eh? Ha! ha! ha!"

"If you please, sir," said Oliver.

"You'd like to be able to make pocket-handkerchiefs as easily as Charley Bates, wouldn't you, my dear?" said Fagin.

"Very much, indeed, if you'll teach me, sir," replied Oliver.

Master Bates saw something so extremely funny in this reply, that he burst into another laugh; which laugh, meeting the coffee he was drinking, and carrying it down the wrong way, very nearly ended in his choking himself.

"He is so very green!" said Charley when he recovered, as an apology to the company for his impolite behaviour.

The Dodger said nothing, but smoothed Oliver's hair over his eyes, and said he'd know better, presently; upon which the old gentleman, observing Oliver's colour rising, changed the subject by asking whether there had been much of a crowd at the execution that morning. This made him wonder more and more; for it was plain from the replies of the two boys that they had both been there; and Oliver naturally wondered how they could possibly have found time to be so very industrious.

When the breakfast was cleared away, the merry old gentleman and the two boys played at a very curious and uncommon game, which was performed in this way. The merry old gentleman, placing a small box in one pocket of his trousers, a note-case in the other, and a watch in his waistcoat pocket, with a watch-chain round his neck, and sticking a diamond pin in his shirt, buttoned his coat tight round him, and putting his glasses and handkerchief in his pockets, walked up and down the room with a stick, in imitation of the manner in which old gentlemen walk about the streets any hour in the day. Sometimes he stopped at the fireplace, and sometimes at the door, pretending that he was staring with all his might into shop windows. At such times, he would look constantly round him, for fear of thieves, and would keep feeling all his pockets in turn, to see that he hadn't lost anything, in such a very funny and natural manner, that Oliver laughed till the tears ran down his face. All this time the two boys followed him closely: getting out of his sight, so quickly, every time he turned round, that it was impossible to follow their movements. At last, the Dodger trod upon his toes, or stepped on his boots accidentally, while Charley Bates fell against him behind: and in that one moment they took from him, with the most extraordinary rapidity, the small box, note-case, watch, chain, shirt-pin, pocket-handkerchief, even the glasses. If the old gentleman felt a hand in any one of his pockets, he cried out where it was; and then the game began all over again.

When this game had been played a great many times, Charley Bates expressed his opinion that it was time to pad the hoof.* This, it occurred to Oliver, must be French for going out; for, directly afterwards, the Dodger and Charley went away together, having been kindly provided by the amiable old Fagin with money to spend.

"There, my dear," said Fagin. "That's a pleasant life, isn't it? They have gone out for the day."

* Pad the hoof = go out, walk (*slang*).

"Have they finished work, sir?" inquired Oliver.

"Yes," said Fagin; "that is, unless they should unexpectedly come across any, when they are out; and they won't neglect it, if they do, my dear, you may depend upon it. Make them your models, my dear. Make them your models," tapping the fire-shovel on the hearth to add force to his words; "do everything they tell you, and take their advice in all matters —especially the Dodger's, my dear. He'll be a great man himself, and will make you one, too, if you copy him. Is my handkerchief hanging out of my pocket, my dear?" said Fagin, stopping suddenly.

"Yes, sir," said Oliver.

"See if you can take it out, without my feeling it: as you saw them do, when we were at play this morning."

Oliver held up the bottom of the pocket with one hand, as he had seen the Dodger hold it, and drew the handkerchief lightly out of it with the other.

"Is it gone?" cried Fagin.

"Here it is, sir," said Oliver, showing it in his hand.

"You're a clever boy, my dear," said the playful old gentleman, patting Oliver on the head approvingly. "I never saw a sharper lad. Here's a shilling for you. If you go on, in this way, you'll be the greatest man of the time. And now come here, and I'll show you how to take the marks out of the handkerchiefs."

Oliver wondered what picking the old gentleman's pocket in play had to do with his chances of being a great man. But, thinking that Fagin, being so much his senior, must know best, he followed him quietly to the table, and was soon deeply engaged in his new study.

II

For many days, Oliver remained in Fagin's room, picking the marks out of the pocket-handkerchiefs (of which a great number were brought home), and sometimes taking part in the game already described: which the two boys and Fagin played, regularly, every morning. At length, he began to long for fresh air, and often earnestly begged the old gentleman to allow him to go out to work, with his two companions.

Oliver was even more anxious to be actively employed after what he had seen of the stern morality of the old gentleman's character. Whenever the Dodger or Charley Bates came home at night empty-handed, he would talk with great emphasis on the misery of idle and lazy habits; and would enforce upon them the necessity of an active life, by sending them supperless to bed. On one occasion, indeed, he even went so far as to knock them both down the stairs; but this was carrying out his moral principles to an unusual extent.

At length, one morning, Oliver was given the permission he had so eagerly asked for. There had been no handkerchiefs to work upon for two or three days, and the dinners had been rather small. Perhaps these were reasons for the old gentleman's giving his permission; but, whether they were or not, he told Oliver he might go, and placed him under the combined protection of Charley Bates, and his friend the Dodger.

The three boys set out; the Dodger with his coat-sleeves rolled up, and his hat at an angle, as usual; Master Bates wandering along with his hands in his pockets; and Oliver between them, wondering where they were going, and what kind of manufacture he would be instructed in first.

The speed at which they went was such a very slow and lazy one, that Oliver soon began to think his companions were going to deceive the old gentleman, by not going to work at all. The Dodger had a vicious habit, too, of pulling the caps from the heads of small boys and throwing them over the nearest railings; while Charley Bates exhibited some very loose ideas concerning the rights of property, by stealing several apples and onions from the stalls in the street, and pushing them into his pockets, which were surprisingly large. These things looked so bad, that Oliver was on the point of announcing his intention of finding his way back, in the best way he could, when his thoughts were suddenly turned to another matter, by a very mysterious change of behaviour on the part of the Dodger.

They were just coming out from a narrow court-yard, not far from the open square, when the Dodger made a sudden stop, and, laying his finger on his lip, drew his companions back again, with the greatest caution.

"What's the matter?", demanded Oliver.

"Hush!" replied the Dodger, "do you see that old cove * at the bookstall?"

"The old gentleman over the way?" said Oliver. "Yes, I see him."

"He'll do," said the Dodger.

"He's a good one," observed Master Charley Bates.

Oliver looked from one to the other, with the greatest surprise; but he was not permitted to make any inquiries, for the two boys walked cautiously across the road, and crept close behind the old gentleman towards whom his attention had been directed. Oliver walked a few steps after them; and, not knowing whether to advance or retire, stood looking on in silent astonishment.

The old gentleman was a very respectable-looking person, with a powdered head and gold-framed glasses. He was dressed in a bottle-green coat with a black velvet collar; wore white trousers, and carried a smart walking-stick under his arm. He had taken up a book from the stall, and there he stood, reading away, as hard as if he were in his arm-chair, in his own study. It is very possible that he imagined he was there, indeed; for it was plain, from his absorption, that he did not see the bookstall, nor the street, nor the boys, nor, in short, anything but the book itself, which he was reading straight through, turning over the page when he got to the bottom, beginning at the top line of the next one, and going regularly on, with the greatest interest and eagerness.

What was Oliver's horror and alarm as he stood a little way off, looking on with his eyes as wide open as they would possibly go, to see the Dodger plunge his hand into the old gentleman's pocket, and draw out a handkerchief; to see

* Cove = man (*slang*).

64

him hand the same to Charley Bates; and finally to see them, both, running away round the corner at full speed!

Immediately the whole mystery of the handkerchiefs, and the watches, and the jewels, and Fagin, rushed upon the boy's mind. He stood, for a moment, with the blood rushing so quickly through his veins from terror, that he felt as if he were in a burning fire; then, confused and frightened, he took to his heels; and, not knowing what he did, ran off as fast as he could put his feet to the ground.

This was all done in a minute's space. At the very moment when Oliver began to run, the old gentleman, putting his hand in his pocket, and missing his handkerchief, turned quickly round. Seeing the boy racing away at such a speed, he very naturally concluded that he was the thief; and, shouting "Stop thief!" with all his might, made off after him, book in hand.

But the old gentleman was not the only person who raised the alarm. The Dodger and Master Bates, unwilling to attract public attention by running down the open street, had merely retired into the very first doorway round the corner. They no sooner heard the cry and saw Oliver running, than, guessing exactly how the matter stood, they promptly rushed out, and, shouting "Stop thief!" too, joined in the pursuit like good citizens.

Not being prepared for this alarm, Oliver became really frightened, so away he went like the wind, with the old gentleman and the two boys roaring and shouting behind him.

"Stop thief! Stop thief!" There is a magic in the sound. The cry is taken up by a hundred voices, and the crowd increases at every turning. Away they fly, splashing through the mud and rushing over the pavements: up go the windows, out run the people, and, joining the pursuers, swell the shout and lend fresh force to the cry, "Stop thief! Stop thief!"

"Stop thief! Stop thief!" There is a passion for hunting deeply implanted in the human breast. One wretched breathless child, panting with exhaustion, terror in his looks, agony in his eyes, strains every nerve to escape from his pursuers; and as they follow on his track, and gain upon him every minute, they greet his decreasing strength with still louder shouts, and scream with joy. "Stop thief!" Yes, stop him for God's sake, if only in mercy!

Stopped at last! A clever blow. He is down upon the pavement; and the crowd eagerly gather round him; each newcomer pushing and struggling with the others to catch a glimpse. "Stand aside!" "Give him a little air!" "Nonsense! he doesn't deserve it." "Where's the gentleman?" "Here he is, coming down the street." "Make room there for the gentleman!" "Is this the boy, sir?" "Yes."

Oliver lay, covered with mud and dust and bleeding from the mouth, looking wildly round at the sea of faces that surrounded him, when the old gentleman was dragged and pushed into the circle by the first of the pursuers.

"Yes," said the gentleman. "I am afraid it is the boy."

"Afraid!" murmured the crowd. "That's a good one!"

"Poor fellow!" said the gentleman; "he has hurt himself."

"I did that, sir," said a great rough fellow, stepping forward, "and I cut my knuckle against his mouth. I stopped him, sir."

The fellow touched his hat with a grin, expecting something for his pains; but the old gentleman, eyeing him with an expression of dislike, looked anxiously round, as if he considered running away himself; which it is very possible he might have attempted to do, and thus have provided another chase, if a police officer (who is generally the last person to arrive in such cases) had not at that moment made his way through the crowd and seized Oliver by the collar.

"Come, get up," said the man, roughly.

"It wasn't me indeed, sir. Indeed, indeed, it was two other boys," said Oliver, clasping his hands passionately and looking round. "They are here somewhere."

"Oh no, they aren't," said the officer, which was quite true; for the Dodger and Charley Bates had slipped off down the first convenient street they came to. "Come on, get up!"

"Don't hurt him," said the old gentleman, moved with pity.

"Oh no, I won't hurt him," replied the officer, tearing his jacket half off his back in proof of this. "Come, I know you: it's no use. Will you stand on your legs, you young devil?"

Oliver, who could hardly stand, made an effort to raise himself on his feet, and was at once pulled along the street by the jacket collar, at a great speed. The gentleman walked on with them by the officer's side; and as many of the crowd as could manage it got a little ahead, and stared back at Oliver from time to time The boys shouted in triumph; and on they went.

The offence had taken place in the district, and indeed in the neighbourhood, of a very notorious London police office. The crowd had only the satisfaction of accompanying Oliver through two or three streets, and down a place called Mutton Hill, when he was led beneath a low archway into the police court. It was a small yard into which they turned, and here they met a stout man with a bunch of whiskers on his face and a bunch of keys in his hand.

"What's the matter now?" said the man carelessly.

"A young thief," replied the man who had Oliver in charge.

"Are you the person that's been robbed, sir?" inquired the man with the keys.

"Yes, I am," replied the old gentleman; "but I am not sure that this boy actually took the handkerchief. I—I would rather not continue with the case."

"Must go before the magistrate now, sir," replied the man. "His worship * will be disengaged in half a minute. Now, young fellow!"

This was an invitation for Oliver to enter through a door which he unlocked as he spoke, and which led into a stone cell. Here his pockets were examined; and nothing being found upon him, he was locked up.

This cell was dark and disgustingly dirty, for it was Monday morning and it had been occupied by six drunken

* His worship = the magistrate.

people, who had been locked up there, since Saturday night. But this is nothing. In our police-stations, men and women are every night kept on the most unimportant charges in these cells, compared with which, those in Newgate Prison, occupied by the most dangerous criminals, tried, found guilty, and under sentence of death, are palaces. Let anyone who doubts this compare the two.

The old gentleman looked almost as miserable as Oliver when the door was locked. He turned with a sigh to the book, which had been the innocent cause of all this disturbance.

"There is something in that boy's face," said the old gentleman to himself as he walked slowly away, tapping his chin with the cover of the book in a thoughtful manner, "something that touches and interests me. Can he be innocent?"

He was roused by a touch on the shoulder, and a request from the man with the keys to follow him into the office. He closed his book hastily, and was at once shown into the majestic presence of the renowned Mr. Fang.

Mr. Fang sat behind a rail at the other end of the room; and on one side of the door was a sort of wooden cage in which poor little Oliver was already placed, trembling very much at the awfulness of the scene.

Mr. Fang was a thin, long-backed, stiff-necked, middle-sized man, with no great quantity of hair, and what he had, growing on the back and sides of his head. His face was stern and very red.

The old gentleman bowed respectfully; and, advancing to the magistrate's desk, gave him his card and said, "That is my name and address, sir." He then withdrew a step or two, and with another polite and gentlemanly bow, waited to be questioned.

Now, it so happened that Mr. Fang was at that moment reading a leading article in a morning newspaper criticising some recent decision of his. He was in a bad temper; and he looked up with an angry frown.

"Who are you?" said Mr. Fang.

The old gentleman pointed, with some surprise, to his card.

"Officer!" said Mr. Fang, throwing the card contemptuously away with the newspaper. "Who is this fellow?"

"My name, sir," said the old gentleman, speaking like a gentleman, "my name, sir, is Brownlow. Permit me to inquire the name of the magistrate who offers such an unnecessary and undeserved insult to a respectable person under the protection of the law." Saying this, Mr. Brownlow looked round the office as if looking for some person who would give him the necessary information.

"Officer!" said Mr. Fang, throwing the paper on one side, "what's this fellow charged with?"

"He's not charged at all, your worship," replied the officer. "He appears against the boy, your worship."

His worship knew this perfectly well; but it was a good excuse for being annoyed.

"Appears against the boy, does he?" said Fang, examining Mr. Brownlow contemptuously from head to foot. "Swear him in."

"Before I am sworn in, I must beg to say one word," said Mr. Brownlow, "and that is, that I really never, without actual experience, could have believed——"

"Hold your tongue, sir!" said Mr. Fang, sharply.

"I will not, sir!" replied the old gentleman.

"Hold your tongue this minute, or I'll have you turned out of the office!" said Mr. Fang. "You're a bad-mannered, impertinent fellow. How dare you insult a magistrate?"

"What!" exclaimed the old gentleman, reddening.

"Swear this person!" said Fang to the clerk. "I'll not hear another word. Swear him."

Mr. Brownlow's indignation was greatly roused; but reflecting perhaps that he might only injure the boy by expressing it, he hid his feelings and allowed himself to be sworn in at once.

"Now," said Fang, "what's the charge against this boy? What have you got to say, sir?"

"I was standing at a bookstall——" Mr. Brownlow began.

"Hold your tongue, sir," said Mr. Fang. "Policeman! Where's the policeman? Here, swear in this policeman. Now, policeman, what is this?"

The policeman, with suitable respect, related how he had taken charge; how he had searched Oliver's pockets and found nothing in them; and how that was all he knew about it.

"Are there any witnesses?" inquired Mr. Fang.

"None, your worship," replied the policeman.

Mr. Fang sat silent for some minutes, and then, turning round to the prosecutor, said furiously:

"Do you mean to state what your complaint against this boy is, man, or do you not? You have been sworn in. Now, if you stand there, refusing to give evidence, I'll punish you for contempt of the court."

With many interruptions, and repeated insults, Mr. Brownlow managed to state his case; remarking that, in the surprise of the moment, he had run after the boy because he saw him running away; and expressing his hope that, if the magistrate should believe him, although not actually the thief, to be connected with thieves, he would deal as mercifully with him as justice would allow.

"He has been hurt already," said the old gentleman in conclusion. "And I fear," he added, with great energy, looking towards the magistrate, "I really fear that he is ill."

"Oh yes, I daresay!" said Mr. Fang, contemptuously. "Come, none of your tricks here, you young villain; they won't help you. What's your name?"

Oliver tried to reply, but his tongue failed him. He was deadly pale, and the whole place seemed turning round and round.

"What's your name, you hardened criminal?" demanded Mr. Fang. "Officer, what's his name?"

This was addressed to an amiable old fellow, in a striped waistcoat, who was standing nearby. He bent over Oliver, and repeated the inquiry; but finding him really unable to understand the question, and knowing that his not replying would only infuriate the magistrate even more, and add to the severity of his sentence, he made a guess.

"He says his name's Tom White, your worship," said this kind-hearted thief-taker.

"Oh, he won't speak out, won't he?" said Fang. "Very well, very well. Where does he live?"

"Where he can, your worship," replied the officer, again pretending to receive Oliver's answer.

"Has he any parents?" inquired Mr. Fang.

"He says they died in his infancy, your worship," replied the officer, knowing it to be the usual reply.

At this point of the inquiry, Oliver raised his head, and, looking round with pitiful eyes, whispered a feeble prayer for a drink of water.

"Nonsense!" said Mr. Fang, "don't try to make a fool of me."

"I think he really is ill, your worship," remarked the officer.

"I know better," said Mr. Fang.

"Take care of him, officer," said the old gentleman, raising his hands instinctively; "he'll fall down."

"Stand away, officer," cried Fang; "let him, if he likes."

Oliver took advantage of the kind permission, and fell to the floor in a faint. The men in the office looked at each other, but no one dared to move.

"I knew he was pretending," said Fang, as if this were undeniable proof of the fact. "Let him lie there; he'll soon be tired of that."

"How do you propose to deal with the case, sir?" inquired the clerk in a low voice.

"Straight away," replied Mr. Fang. "He goes to prison for three months—hard labour of course. Clear the office."

The door was opened for this purpose, and a couple of men were preparing to carry the unconscious boy to his cell, when a middle-aged, respectable-looking man, clad in an old suit of black, rushed hastily into the office, and advanced towards the far end of the room.

"Stop, stop! Don't take him away! For Heaven's sake, stop a moment!" he cried, breathless with haste.

"What is this? Who is this? Turn this man out. Clear the office!" cried Mr. Fang.

"I will speak," cried the man; "I will not be turned out. I saw it all. I keep the bookstall. I demand to be sworn in. I will not be put off. Mr. Fang, you must hear me. You must not refuse, sir."

The man was right. His manner was determined, and the matter was growing rather too serious to be kept quiet.

"Swear the man in," muttered Mr. Fang, with a very bad grace. "Now, man, what have you got to say?"

"This," said the man; "I saw three boys, two others and the prisoner here, standing on the opposite side of the street, when this gentleman was reading. The robbery was committed by another boy. I saw it done; and I saw that this boy was perfectly astonished and surprised by it." Having by this time recovered a little breath, the worthy bookstall keeper proceeded to relate, in a more connected manner, the exact circumstances of the robbery.

"Why didn't you come here before?" said Fang, after a pause.

"I hadn't anyone to mind the shop," replied the man. "Everybody who could have helped me had joined in the pursuit. I could get nobody till five minutes ago; and I've run here all the way."

"The prosecutor was reading, was he?" inquired Fang, after another pause.

"Yes," replied the man. "The very book he has in his hand."

"Oh, that book, eh?" said Fang. "Is it paid for?"

"No, it is not," replied the man, with a smile.

"Dear me, I forgot all about it!" exclaimed the absent-minded old gentleman, innocently.

"A nice person to make a charge against a poor boy!" said Fang, with an amusing effort to look merciful. "I consider, sir, that you have taken possession of that book under very suspicious and doubtful circumstances; and you may think yourself very fortunate that the owner of the property refuses to prosecute. Let this be a lesson to you, my man, or the law

72

will overtake you yet. The boy is released. Clear the office."

"Good Heavens!" cried the old gentleman, bursting out with the fury he had controlled for so long, "Good Heavens! I'll——"

"Clear the office!" said the magistrate. "Officers, do you hear? Clear the office!"

The order was obeyed; and the indignant Mr. Brownlow was led out, with the book in one hand and the walking-stick in the other, in a perfect state of anger and defiance. He reached the yard, and his passion disappeared in a moment. Little Oliver Twist lay on his back on the pavement, with his shirt unbuttoned, and his forehead bathed with water, his face a deadly white, and his whole body shaking with cold and fear.

"Poor boy, poor boy!" said Mr. Brownlow, bending over him. "Call a coach, somebody, please. Directly!"

A coach was brought, and Oliver, having been carefully laid on one seat, the old gentleman got in and sat down on the other.

"May I accompany you?" said the bookstall keeper, looking in.

"Bless me, yes, my dear sir," said Mr. Brownlow quickly. "I forgot you. Dear, dear! I have this unhappy book still! Jump in. Poor fellow! There's no time to lose."

The bookstall keeper got into the coach; and away they drove.

[The kind-hearted Mr. Brownlow takes Oliver into his home and, for a time at any rate, Oliver's troubles are over.]

DOTHEBOYS HALL (from *Nicholas Nickleby*)

I

[The Nickleby family are in need of money and, in order to support his mother and sister, Nicholas has, with some hesitation, taken the post of assistant schoolmaster to Mr. Squeers at Dotheboys Hall in Yorkshire. They have just arrived there after a long journey from London.]

"JUMP OUT," said Squeers. "Hallo, there! Come and put this horse up. Be quick, will you!"

While the schoolmaster was giving these and other impatient commands, Nicholas had time to observe that the school was a long, cold-looking house, one storey high, with a few straggling outbuildings behind, and a barn and stable next to them. After a minute or two, the noise of somebody unlocking the yard-gate was heard, and presently a tall, thin boy, with a lamp in his hand, came out.

"Is that you, Smike?" cried Squeers.

"Yes, sir," replied the boy.

"Then why the devil didn't you come before?"

"Please, sir, I fell asleep over the fire," answered Smike, humbly.

"Fire! What fire? Where's there a fire?" demanded the schoolmaster, sharply.

"Only in the kitchen, sir," replied the boy. "Mrs. Squeers said as I was sitting up, I might go in there for a warm."

"She's a fool," retorted Squeers. "You'd have been a good deal more wide awake in the cold, I'm sure."

By this time Mr. Squeers had got down, and after ordering the boy to see to the pony and to take care that he hadn't any more corn that night, he told Nicholas to wait at the front door a minute, while he went round and let him in.

Many unpleasant doubts, which had been crowding upon Nicholas during the whole journey, returned to his mind with even greater force when he was left alone. His great distance from home and the impossibility of reaching it, except on foot, was alarming; and as he looked up at the dreary house and dark windows, and upon the wild country round covered with snow, he felt his heart and spirit sinking more than he had ever experienced before.

"Now, then!" cried Squeers, poking his head out at the front door. "Where are you, Nickleby?"

"Here, sir," replied Nicholas.

"Come in, then," said Squeers; "the wind blows in at this door enough to knock a man off his legs."

Nicholas sighed, and hurried in. Mr. Squeers, having locked the door to keep it shut, showed him into a small room poorly furnished with a few chairs, a yellow map hung against the wall, and a couple of tables, one of which bore some preparations for supper.

They had not been in this room a couple of minutes when a female rushed into the room, and, seizing Mr. Squeers by the throat, gave him two loud kisses, one close after the other, like a postman's knock. The lady, who had a large bony figure, was about half a head taller than Mr. Squeers, and was dressed in a coarse cotton nightdress, with her hair in curl-papers; she had also a dirty nightcap on, fastened by a yellow cotton handkerchief, which was tied under the chin.

"How is my Squeery?" said this lady, in a playful manner and a very hoarse voice.

"Quite well, my love," replied Squeers. "How are the cows?"

"All right, every one of them," answered the lady.

"And the pigs?" said Squeers.

"As well as they were when you went away."

"Ah! That's a blessing," said Squeers, taking off his overcoat. "The boys are all as they were, I suppose?"

"Oh yes, they're well enough," replied Mrs. Squeers, irritably. "That young Pitcher's had a fever."

"No!" exclaimed Squeers. "Curse that boy; he's always doing something of that sort."

"There never was such a boy, I do believe," said Mrs.

Squeers. "Whatever he has is always catching, too. I say it's obstinacy, and nothing shall ever persuade me that it isn't. I'd beat it out of him, and I told you that six months ago."

"So you did, my love," replied Squeers. "We'll try what can be done."

During this conversation, Nicholas had stood, awkwardly enough, in the middle of the room, not knowing whether he was expected to go outside or to remain where he was. He was now relieved from his embarrassment by Mr. Squeers.

"This is the new young man, my dear," said that gentleman.

"Oh," replied Mrs. Squeers, nodding her head at Nicholas, and eyeing him coldly from top to toe.

"He'll take a meal with us to-night," said Squeers, "and go among the boys to-morrow morning. You can give him a bed for to-night, can't you?"

"We must manage it somehow," replied the lady. "You don't much mind how you sleep, I suppose, sir?"

"No, indeed," replied Nicholas; "I am not particular."

"That's lucky," said Mrs. Squeers. And as the lady's humour was considered to lie chiefly in retort, Mr. Squeers laughed heartily, and seemed to expect that Nicholas should do the same.

After some further conversation between the master and mistress, concerning the success of Mr. Squeers's trip, and the people who had paid, and the people who had failed to pay, a young servant girl brought in a Yorkshire pie and some cold beef, which being set upon the table, the boy Smike appeared with a jug of beer.

Mr. Squeers was emptying his overcoat pockets of letters to different boys, and other small documents which he had brought down in them. The boy glanced with an anxious and timid expression at the papers, as if with a faint hope that one among them might refer to him. The look was a very painful one and went to Nicholas's heart at once, for it told a long and very sad history.

It caused him to consider the boy more attentively, and he was surprised to observe the extraordinary mixture of garments which he wore. Although he could not have been less than eighteen or nineteen years old, and was tall for that age, he wore a suit such as is usually put on very little boys, and which was most absurdly short in the arms and legs. He had a very large pair of boots, which might have been once worn by some stout farmer, but were now too torn and ragged for a beggar. Heaven knows how long he had been there, but he still wore the same clothes which he had when he first went there; for round his neck was a ragged child's collar, only half-hidden by a coarse, man's scarf. He limped; and as he pretended to be busy in arranging the table, glanced at the letters with a look so keen, and yet so weary and hopeless, that Nicholas could hardly bear to watch him.

"What are you doing there, Smike?" cried Mrs. Squeers; "let things alone, can't you."

"Eh!" said Squeers, looking up. "Oh! it's you, is it?"

"Yes, sir," replied the youth, pressing his hands together, as if to control by force the nervous wandering of his fingers; "is there——"

"Well!" said Squeers.

"Have you—did anybody—has nothing been heard—about me?"

"Not a word," said Squeers, irritably, "and never will be. Now, this is a fine state of affairs, isn't it, that you should have been left here all these years and no money paid after the first six—and no information to be got who you belong to? It's a fine state of affairs that I should have to feed a great fellow like you, and never hope to get one penny for it, isn't it?"

The boy put his hand to his head as if he were making an effort to remember something, and then, looking stupidly at his questioner, gradually broke into a smile, and limped away.

"I'll tell you what, Squeers," remarked his wife as the door closed, "I think that young fellow's going mad."

"I hope not," said the schoolmaster; "for he's a useful fellow out of doors, and worth his meat and drink, anyway. I should think he'd be clever enough for us though, if he was. But come; let's have supper, for I'm hungry and tired, and want to get to bed."

This reminder brought in a steak for Mr. Squeers, who speedily proceeded to eat it with enjoyment. Nicholas drew up his chair, but his appetite was effectively taken away.

"How's the steak, Squeers?" said Mrs. S.

"Tender as a lamb," replied Squeers. "Have a bit?"

"I couldn't eat anything," replied his wife. "What'll the young man have, my dear?"

"Whatever he likes that's here," replied Squeers, in a most unusual burst of generosity.

"What do you say, Mr. Knuckleboy?" inquired Mrs. Squeers.

"I'll have a little of the pie, if you please," replied Nicholas. "A very little, for I'm not hungry."

"Well, it's a pity to cut the pie if you're not hungry, isn't it?" said Mrs. Squeers. "Will you try a bit of the beef?"

"Whatever you please," replied Nicholas, absent-mindedly; "it's all the same to me."

Mrs. Squeers looked vastly pleased on receiving this reply; and nodding to Squeers, as much as to say that she was glad to find the young man knew his place, helped Nicholas to a slice of meat with her own fair hands.

"Beer, Squeery?" inquired the lady, winking and frowning to give him to understand that the question asked was, whether Nicholas should have beer and not whether he (Squeers) should take any.

"Certainly," said Squeers, re-telegraphing in the same manner; "a glassful."

So Nicholas had a glassful, and being occupied with his own thoughts drank it in happy innocence of the meaning of all these remarks.

"Uncommonly juicy steak that," said Squeers, as he laid down his knife and fork, after using them in silence for some time.

"It's the best meat," replied his lady. "I bought a good large piece of it myself for——"

"For what?" exclaimed Squeers, hastily. "Not for the——"

"No, no, not for them," answered Mrs. Squeers; "for when
you came home. Good heavens! you didn't think I could
have made such a mistake as that?"

A page from the original manuscript of Nicholas Nickleby

"Upon my word, my dear, I didn't know what you were going to say," said Squeers, who had turned pale.

"You needn't make yourself uncomfortable," remarked his wife, laughing heartily. "To think that I should be so stupid. Well!"

This part of the conversation was rather difficult to understand, but there were popular tales in the neighbourhood that Mr. Squeers, being amiably opposed to cruelty to animals, not infrequently bought for the boys' food the bodies of cattle who had died a natural death. Possibly he was afraid of having unintentionally eaten some tasty joint intended for the young gentlemen.

Supper being over, and removed by a small servant-girl with a hungry eye, Mrs. Squeers retired to lock it up, and also to take to a safe place the clothes of the five boys who had just arrived, and who were half-way up the troublesome steps which lead to death's door, as a result of exposure to the cold. They were then treated to a light supper of porridge, and packed away, side by side, in a small bed, to warm each other, and dream of a substantial meal, with something hot after it, if their fancies went that way, which it is not at all improbable they did.

Mr. Squeers treated himself to a large glass of brandy and water, and his amiable wife mixed Nicholas the ghost of a small glassful of the same drink. This done, Mr. and Mrs. Squeers drew their chairs close to the fire, and sitting with their feet on the hearth, talked confidentially in whispers.

At length Mr. Squeers yawned widely, and remarked that it was high time to go to bed; upon which signal Mrs. Squeers and the girl dragged in a small straw mattress and a couple of blankets, and arranged them into a bed for Nicholas.

"We'll put you into your proper bedroom to-morrow, Nickleby," said Squeers, thinking hard. "There's Jennings, little Bolder, Graymarsh, and what's-his-name."

"So there is," replied Mrs. Squeers. "Yes! Brooks's bed is full."

"Full," thought Nicholas; "I should think it was."

"There's a place somewhere, I know," said Squeers; "but

80

I can't at this moment call to mind where it is. However, we'll have that all setttled to-morrow. Good night, Nickleby. Seven o'clock in the morning, mind."

"I shall be ready, sir," replied Nicholas. "Good night."

"I'll come in myself and show you where the well is," said Squeers. "You'll always find a little bit of soap in the kitchen window; that belongs to you."

Nicholas opened his eyes, but not his mouth; and Squeers was again going away when he once more turned back.

"I don't know, I'm sure," he said, "whose towel to put you on; but if you'll make do with something else to-morrow morning, Mrs. Squeers will arrange that in the course of the day——. My dear, don't forget."

"I'll take care," replied Mrs. Squeers, "and mind you take care, young man, and get the first wash. The teacher ought always to have it; but they get the better of him if they can."

Mr. Squeers then whispered to Mrs. Squeers to bring away the brandy-bottle, in case Nicholas should help himself in the night; and the lady having seized it with great haste, they retired together.

Nicholas being left alone, walked up and down the room in a condition of much agitation and excitement; but growing gradually calmer, sat down in a chair, and resolved that, whatever happened, he would try for a time to bear whatever wretchedness might be in store for him, and that remembering the helplessness of his mother and sister, he would not desert them in their need. He grew less despairing and (so optimistic and confident is youth)—even hoped that affairs at Dotheboys Hall might yet prove better than they promised.

II

The next morning, Nicholas's dreams were interrupted by the faint glow of a candle before his eyes, and a voice he had no difficulty in recognising as part and parcel of Mr. Squeers informed him that it was time to rise.

"Past seven, Nickleby," said Mr. Squeers.

"Has morning come already?" asked Nicholas, sitting up in bed.

"Ah! that it has," replied Squeers; "and ready iced too. Now, Nickleby, come; get up, will you?"

Nicholas needed no further persuasion, but got up at once, and proceeded to dress himself by the light of the candle which Mr. Squeers carried in his hand.

"Here's a fine thing," said that gentleman: "the pump's frozen."

"Indeed" said Nicholas, not much interested in the news.

"Yes," replied Squeers. "You can't wash yourself this morning."

"Not wash myself!" exclaimed Nicholas.

"No, not a bit of it," answered Squeers, sharply. "So you must be content with giving yourself a dry polish till we break the ice in the well and can get a bucketful out for the boys. Don't stand staring at me, but do look sharp, will you?"

Making no further remarks, Nicholas pulled on his clothes. Squeers meanwhile drew back the curtains and blew the candle out, when the voice of his amiable wife was heard outside, demanding admission.

"Come in, my love," said Squeers.

Mrs. Squeers came in, still dressed in her nightclothes and an old nightcap, which she wore, with much ease and lightness, on the top of her head.

"Curse the things," said the lady, opening the cupboard; "I can't find the school spoon anywhere."

"Never mind, my dear," remarked Squeers, in a comforting manner; "it's of no importance."

"No importance; why, how you talk!" retorted Mrs. Squeers, sharply; "isn't it brimstone morning?"

"I forgot, my dear," replied Squeers. "Yes, it certainly is. We purify the boys' blood now and then, Nickleby."

"Purify fiddlesticks' ends,"* said his lady. "Don't think, young man, that we go to the expense of brimstone and treacle just to purify them; because if you think we carry on

* "Fiddlesticks' ends" is a colloquial expression meaning "nonsense."

the business in that way, you'll find yourself mistaken, and so I tell you plainly."

"My dear!" said Squeers, frowning.

"Oh, nonsense," replied Mrs. Squeers. "If the young man comes to be a teacher here, let him understand at once that we don't want any foolery about the boys. They have the brimstone and treacle, partly because if they hadn't something or other in the way of medicine, they'd be always falling ill and giving a world of trouble, and partly because it spoils their appetites and comes cheaper than breakfast and dinner. So it does them good at the same time, and that's fair enough, I'm sure."

"A most invaluable woman that, Nickleby," said Squeers, when his wife had hurried away.

"Indeed, sir!" remarked Nicholas.

"I don't know her equal," said Squeers, "I do not know her equal. That woman, Nickleby, is always the same— always the same energetic, lively, active, saving creature that you see her now."

Nicholas sighed involuntarily at the thought of the agreeable domestic outlook thus opened to him; but Squeers was, fortunately, too much occupied with his own thoughts to notice it.

"I always say, when I am up in London," continued Squeers, "that to those boys she is a mother. But she is more than a mother to them—ten times more; she does things for those boys, Nickleby, that I don't believe half the mothers in the world would do for their own sons."

"I should think they would not, sir," answered Nicholas.

Now the fact was that both Mr. and Mrs. Squeers regarded the boys as their natural enemies; or, in other words, they firmly believed that their business and profession was to get as much from every boy as could possibly be screwed out of him. On this point they were both agreed, and behaved accordingly. The only difference between them was that Mrs. Squeers fought against the enemy openly and fearlessly, and that Squeers covered his villainy, even at home, with something of his habitual deceit; as if he really had an idea of some day or other being able to deceive himself and persuade his own mind that he was a very good fellow.

"But come," said Squeers, interrupting the progress of some thoughts of this kind in the mind of his assistant, "let's go to the schoolroom; and lend me a hand with my school coat, will you?"

Nicholas assisted his master to put on an old shooting-jacket, which he took down from a nail on the wall; and Squeers, arming himself with his cane, led the way across the yard to a door in the rear of the house.

"There," said the schoolmaster, as they stepped in together, "this is our shop, Nickleby."

It was such a crowded scene, and there were so many objects to attract attention, that at first Nicholas stared about him, really without seeing anything at all. By degrees, however, the place showed itself to be a bare and dirty room, with a couple of broken windows, a tenth part of which might be of glass, the remainder being stopped up with old copy-books and paper. There were a couple of long, old, broken-down desks, cut and inked, and damaged in every possible way; two or three wooden seats; a separate desk for Squeers, and another for his assistant. The walls were so dirty and discoloured that it was impossible to tell whether they had ever been touched with paint or whitewash.

But the pupils—the young noblemen! How the last faint traces of hope of any good to be gained from his efforts in this awful place faded from the mind of Nicholas as he looked in dismay around! Pale and worn faces, and thin bony figures, children with faces of old men, boys with irons upon their distorted limbs, boys of arrested growth, and others whose long, thin legs would hardly bear their stooping bodies, all met together; there were sore eyes, the twisted lip, the crooked foot, and every ugliness or distortion that told of young lives which, from the earliest dawn of infancy, had been one horrible endurance of cruelty and neglect. There were little faces which should have been handsome, darkened with the frown of long, dreary, hopeless suffering; there was childhood with the light of its eye darkened, its beauty gone, and its helplessness alone remaining; there were vicious-faced boys, with heavy eyes, like criminals in a prison; and there were young creatures on whom the sins of their frail parents had descended, weeping even for the harsh nurses they had known. With every kindly sympathy and affection destroyed in its birth, with every young and healthy feeling beaten and starved down, with every revengeful passion that can spread like a disease in swollen hearts, eating its evil way in silence, what horrors were breeding here!

And yet this scene, painful as it was, had its grotesque features, which in a less interested observer than Nicholas might have caused a smile. Mrs. Squeers stood at one of the desks, presiding over an immense basin of brimstone and treacle, of which delicious mixture she gave a large helping to each boy in turn, using for the purpose an enormous wooden spoon, which widened every young gentleman's mouth considerably—they being all obliged, under threat of heavy punishment, to take in the whole of the spoon at one go. In another corner, crowded close together for companionship, were the little boys who had arrived on the previous night, three of them in very large, and two in old, trousers. At no great distance from these was seated the young son and heir of Mr. Squeers—a striking likeness of his father—kicking with great energy, in the hands of Smike, who was fitting him with a pair of new boots that looked most suspiciously like those which the smallest of the little boys had worn on the journey down—as the little boy himself seemed to think, for he was regarding them with a look of most unhappy astonishment.

Besides these, there was a long row of boys waiting, with faces of unpleasant anticipation, to be treacled; and another lot, who had just had their spoonful, making a variety of faces, that showed anything but satisfaction. All of them were dressed in such mixed and extraordinary garments as would have been irresistibly ridiculous, but for the disgusting appearance of dirt and disease with which they were associated.

"Now," said Squeers, giving the desk a great knock with his cane, which made half the little boys nearly jump out of their boots, "is that doctoring over?"

"Just over," said Mrs. Squeers, choking the last boy in her hurry, and tapping the crown of his head with the wooden spoon to restore him. "Here, you Smike; take it away now. Look sharp!"

Smike limped out with the basin, and Mrs. Squeers having called up a little boy with a curly head, and wiped her hands upon it, hurried out after him into a kind of wash-house, where there was a small fire and a large kettle, together with a number of little wooden bowls which were ranged upon a board.

Into these bowls Mrs. Squeers, assisted by the hungry servant, poured a brown mixture which looked like water and pin-cushions without the covers and was called porridge. A tiny piece of brown bread was put into each bowl, and when they had eaten their porridge by means of the bread, the boys ate the bread itself, and had finished their breakfast. Then Mr. Squeers said, in a solemn voice, "For what we have received may the Lord make us truly thankful," and went away to his own.

Nicholas filled his stomach with a bowl of porridge, in case he should be inconveniently hungry when there was nothing to eat. Having also swallowed a slice of bread and butter, given to him because of his higher position, he sat down to wait for school-time.

He could not help noticing how silent and sad the boys all seemed to be. There was none of the noise and shouting of a schoolroom, none of its cheerful play or hearty mirth. The children sat crouching and shivering together, and seemed to lack the spirit to move about. The only pupil who showed the slightest desire for movement or playfulness was Master Squeers, and as his chief amusement was to tread upon the other boys' toes in his new boots, his flow of spirits was rather disagreeable than otherwise.

After about half an hour's delay, Mr. Squeers appeared again, and the boys took their places and their books, each of the latter being shared by about eight pupils. A few minutes having passed, during which Mr. Squeers looked very thoughtful, as if he knew perfectly what was inside all the books, and could say every word of their contents by heart if he only chose to take the trouble, that gentleman called up the first class.

Half a dozen wretched little boys stood in a row in front of the schoolmaster's desk, and one of them placed a torn and dirty book beneath his learned eye.

"This is the first class in English spelling and philosophy, Nickleby," said Squeers, signing for Nicholas to stand beside him. "Now, then, where's the first boy?"

"Please, sir, he's cleaning the back-room window," said one of the boys, the head, for the moment, of the philosophical class.

"So he is, to be sure," replied Squeers. "We use the practical method of teaching, Nickleby—the regular education system. C-l-e-a-n, clean, verb active, to make bright. W-i-n, win, d-e-r, der, winder, an opening for the light. When the boy knows this out of the book, he goes and does it. Where's the second boy?"

"Please, sir, he's weeding the garden," replied a small voice.

"To be sure," said Squeers, by no means put out. "So he is. B-o-t, bot, t-i-n, tin, bottin, n-e-y, ney, botany, common noun, a knowledge of plants. When he has learned that botany means a knowledge of plants, he goes and knows them. That's our system, Nickleby; what do you think of it?"

"It's a very useful one, at any rate," answered Nicholas.

"I believe you," said Squeers, not noticing the irony of his assistant. "Third boy, what's a horse?"

"A beast, sir," replied the boy.

"So it is," said Squeers. "Isn't it, Nickleby?"

"I believe there is no doubt of that, sir," answered Nicholas.

"Of course there isn't," said Squeers. "As you're perfect in that, go and look after my horse, and rub him down well, or I'll rub you down. The rest of the class go and draw water up, till somebody tells you to stop; for it's washing-day to-morrow, and they want the boilers filled."

Saying this, he dismissed the first class to their experiments in practical philosophy, and eyed Nicholas with a look, half cunning and half doubtful, as if he were not altogether certain what he might think of him by this time.

"That's the way we do it, Nickleby," he said, after a pause. Nicholas said he saw it was.

"And a very good way it is, too," said Squeers. "Now, just take those fourteen little boys and hear them reading, because, you know, you must begin to be useful. Idling about here won't do."

Mr. Squeers said this as if it had suddenly occurred to him, either that he must not say too much to his assistant, or that his assistant did not say enough to him in praise of the school. The children arranged themselves in a semi-circle round the new master, and he was soon listening to their dull, monotonous, hesitating reading of those stories which are to be found in the more antiquated spelling books.

In this exciting occupation the morning passed slowly by. At one o'clock, the boys having previously had their appetites thoroughly taken away by thin soup and potatoes, sat down in the kitchen to some hard salt beef, of which Nicholas was permitted to take his share to his own desk, to eat it there in peace. After this, there was another hour of crouching in the schoolroom and shivering with cold, and then school began again.

It was Mr. Squeers's custom to call the boys together, and make a sort of report, after every half-yearly visit to London, regarding the relations and friends he had seen, the news he had heard, the letters he had brought down, the bills which had been paid, the accounts which had been left unpaid, and so on. This solemn proceeding always took place in the afternoon of the ·day following his return, perhaps because the boys gained strength of mind from the morning's wait, or possibly Mr. Squeers gained greater sternness and firmness from certain warm drinks which he was accustomed to take after his early dinner.

Whatever the reason, the boys were called in from window, garden, stable, and cow-yard, and the school were gathered together in full strength, when Mr. Squeers, with a small bundle of papers in his hand, and Mrs. S. following with a pair of canes, entered the room and ordered silence.

"Let any boy speak a word without permission," said Mr. Squeers, mildly, "and I'll take the skin off his back."

This special announcement had the desired effect, and immediately there fell a death-like silence, in the midst of which Mr. Squeers went on to say:

"Boys, I've been to London, and have returned to my family and you as strong and well as ever."

According to half-yearly custom, the boys gave three feeble cheers at this refreshing information.

"I have seen the parents of some boys," continued Squeers, turning over his papers, "and they're so glad to hear how their sons are getting on that there's no chance at all of their leaving here, which, of course, is a very pleasant thing to think of, for all concerned."

Two or three hands went to two or three eyes when Squeers said this, but the greater part of the young gentlemen, having no particular parents to speak of, were wholly uninterested in the thing one way or other.

"I have had disappointments to fight again," said Squeers, looking very grim. "Bolder's father was two pound ten short. Where is Bolder?"

"Here he is, please, sir," answered twenty eager voices. Boys are very like men, to be sure.

"Come here, Bolder," said Squeers.

An unhealthy-looking boy, with sores all over his hands, stepped from his place to the master's desk, and raised his eyes appealing to Squeers's face, his own quite white from the rapid beating of his heart.

"Bolder," said Squeers, speaking very slowly, for he was considering how to deal with him—"Bolder, if your father thinks that because—why, what's this, sir?"

As Squeers spoke, he caught hold of the boy's hand by the

sleeve of his jacket, and examined it with an aspect of horror and disgust.

"What do you call this, sir?" demanded the schoolmaster, giving him a cut with the cane to hasten the reply.

"I can't help it, indeed, sir," answered the boy, crying. "They will come; it's the dirty work, I think, sir—at least I don't know what it is, sir, but it's not my fault."

"Bolder," said Squeers, turning up his sleeves, and moistening the palm of his right hand to get a good grip of the cane, "you're an incurable young villain; and as the last whipping did you no good, we must see what another will do towards beating it out of you."

With this, and taking no notice whatever of a pitiful cry for mercy, Mr. Squeers seized the boy and caned him soundly, not leaving off, indeed, until his arm was tired out.

"There," said Mr. Squeers, when he had quite done, "rub away as hard as you like, you won't rub that off in a hurry. Oh! you won't stop that noise, won't you? Put him out, Smike."

The poor slave knew better from long experience than to hesitate about obeying, so he pushed the victim out by a side door; and Mr. Squeers sat down again on his own stool, supported by Mrs. Squeers, who occupied another at his side.

"Now, let us see," said Squeers. "A letter for Cobbey. Stand up, Cobbey."

Another boy stood up, and eyed the letter very hard while Squeers read it silently.

"Oh!" said Squeers. "Cobbey's grandmother is dead, and his uncle John has taken to drink, which is all the news his sister sends, except eighteenpence, which will just pay for that broken square of glass. Mrs. Squeers, my dear, will you take the money?"

The worthy lady pocketed the eighteenpence with a most business-like air, and Squeers passed on to the next boy, as coolly as possible.

"Graymarsh," said Squeers, "he's the next. Stand up, Graymarsh."

Another boy stood up, and the schoolmaster glanced through the letter as before.

"Graymarsh's aunt," said Squeers, "is very glad to hear he's so well and happy, and sends her respectful compliments to Mrs. Squeers, and thinks she must be an angel. She also thinks Mr. Squeers is too good for this world, but hopes he may be long spared to carry on the business. Would have sent the two pairs of stockings as desired, but is short of money, so sends a Bible lesson instead, and hopes Graymarsh will put his trust in God. Hopes, above all, that he will study in everything to please Mr. and Mrs. Squeers, and look upon them as his only friends; and that he will love Master Squeers; and not object to sleeping five in a bed, which no Christian should. Ah!" said Squeers, folding it up. "A delightful letter, very affecting indeed."

He proceeded with the business by calling out "Mobbs"; upon which another boy rose, and Graymarsh returned to his seat.

"Mobbs's step-mother," said Squeers, "had to go to her bed on hearing that he wouldn't eat fat, and has been very ill ever since. She wishes to know by early post where he expects to go if he quarrels with his food; and with what feelings he could turn up his nose at the potato soup after his good master had asked a blessing on it. She is sorry to find he is discontented, which is very sinful, and hopes Mr. Squeers will beat him into a happier state of mind; because of this she has also stopped his halfpenny a week pocket-money, and given away to someone else a double-bladed knife with a corkscrew in it which she had really bought for him."

"A discontented state of feelings," said Squeers, after a terrible pause, during which he had moistened the palm of his right hand again, "won't do; cheerfulness and contentment must be kept up. Mobbs, come to me!"

Mobbs moved slowly towards the desk, rubbing his eyes in anticipation of good cause for doing so; and he soon afterwards retired by the side door, with as good cause as a boy need have.

Mr. Squeers then proceeded to open a varied collection of

letters, some enclosing money, which Mrs. Squeers "took care of," and others referring to small articles of clothing such as caps and so on, all of which the same lady stated to be too large or two small, thinking of nobody but young Squeers, who, so it seemed, had limbs of a most convenient size, since everything that came into the school fitted him to a nicety. His head, in particular, must have been extraordinarily elastic, for hats and caps of all sizes were alike to him.

This business finished with, a few slovenly lessons were given, and Squeers retired to his fireside, leaving Nicholas to take care of the boys in the schoolroom, which was very cold, and where a meal of bread and cheese was served out shortly after dark.

There was a small stove at that corner of the room which was nearest to the master's desk, and by it Nicholas sat down, so down-hearted and miserable because of his position, that if death could have come upon him at that time he would have been almost happy to meet it.

But for the present his mind was made up, and the decision he had made the previous night remained undisturbed. He had written to his mother and sister, announcing the safe conclusion of his journey, but saying little about Dotheboys Hall, and saying that little as cheerfully as he possibly could. He hoped that by remaining where he was, he might do some good, even there.

As he was absorbed in these thoughts, he all at once saw the upturned face of Smike, who was on his knees before the stove, picking a few scattered ashes from the hearth and putting them on the fire. He had paused to steal a look at Nicholas, and when he saw that he was observed, shrunk back, as if expecting a blow.

"You need not fear me," said Nicholas, kindly. "Are you cold?"

"N-no."

"You are shivering."

"I am not cold," replied Smike, quickly. "I'm used to it."

There was such an obvious fear of giving offence in his manner, and he was such a timid, broken-spirited creature, that Nicholas could not help exclaiming, "Poor fellow!"

If he had struck the poor wretch, Smike would have crept away without a word; but now he burst into tears.

"Oh dear, oh dear!" he cried, covering his face with his cracked and bony hands. "My heart will break—it will, it will!"

"Calm yourself," said Nicholas, laying his hand upon his shoulder. "Be a man; you are nearly by years, God help you."

"By years!" cried Smike. "Oh dear, dear, how many of them! How many of them since I was a little child, younger than any that are here now! Where are they all?"

"Whom do you speak of?" inquired Nicholas, wishing to rouse the poor half-witted creature to reason. "Tell me."

"My friends," he replied, "myself—my—oh, what sufferings mine have been!"

"There is always hope," said Nicholas; he didn't know what to say.

"No," replied the other, "no, none for me. Do you remember the boy that died here?"

"I was not here, you know," said Nicholas, gently; "but what of him?"

"Why," replied the youth, drawing closer to his questioner's side, "I was with him at night, and when it was all silent he cried no more for friends he wished to come and sit with him, but began to see faces round his bed that came from home: he said they smiled, and talked to him, and he died at last lifting his head to kiss them. Do you hear?"

"Yes, yes," answered Nicholas.

"What faces will smile on me when I die?" cried the boy, shivering. "Who will talk to me in those long nights? They cannot come from home; they would frighten me if they did, for I don't know what it is, and shouldn't know them. Pain and fear, pain and fear, for me, alive or dead. No hope, no hope!"

The bell rang for bed; and the boy, falling back at the sound into his usual listless state, crept away as if anxious to avoid notice. It was with a heavy heart that Nicholas soon afterwards retired—no, not retired; there was no retirement there—followed to his dirty and crowded bedroom.

III

[A few weeks later.]

The cold, feeble dawn of a January morning was stealing in at the windows of the common sleeping-room, when Nicholas, raising himself on his arm, looked among the sleeping forms which on every side surrounded him.

It needed a quick eye to recognise, from among the crowded mass of sleepers, the form of any particular individual. As they lay closely packed together, covered, for warmth's sake, with their torn and ragged clothes, little could be distinguished but the sharp outlines of pale faces, over which the dim light threw the same dull, heavy colour, with here and there a thin arm stretched forth, its thinness hidden by no covering, but fully exposed to view, in all its pitiful ugliness. They looked more like dead bodies than living creatures. A few—and these were among the youngest of the children—slept peacefully on, with smiles upon their faces, dreaming perhaps of home; but every now and then a deep and heavy sigh, breaking the stillness of the room, announced that some new sleeper had awakened to the misery of another day, and as morning took the place of night, the smiles gradually faded away with the friendly darkness which had given them birth.

Nicholas looked sorrowfully upon this scene, and then, not noticing something he usually saw, he had half-risen from his bed, when the voice of Squeers was heard, calling from the bottom of the stairs.

"Now then," cried that gentleman, "are you going to sleep all day, up there?"

"You lazy dogs!" added Mrs. Squeers, finishing the sentence.

"We shall be down directly, sir," replied Nicholas.

"Down directly!" said Squeers. "Ah! you had better be

94

down directly, or I'll be down upon some of you even sooner. Where's that Smike?"

Nicholas looked hurriedly round again, but made no answer.

"Smike!" shouted Squeers.

"Do you want your head broken in a fresh place, Smike?" demanded his amiable lady.

Still there was no reply, and still Nicholas stared about him, as did the greater part of the boys, who were by this time roused.

"Curse his impertinence," muttered Squeers, striking the stair impatiently with his cane. "Nickleby!"

"Well, sir."

"Send that obstinate villain down; don't you hear me calling?"

"He is not here, sir," replied Nicholas.

"Don't tell me a lie," retorted the schoolmaster. "He is."

"He is not," retorted Nicholas, angrily, "don't tell me one."

"We shall soon see about that," said Mr. Squeers, rushing upstairs. "I'll find him, I promise you."

With which Mr. Squeers hurried into the bedroom, and swinging his cane in the air ready for a blow, dashed in to the corner where the thin body of the poor wretch was usually stretched at night. The cane descended harmlessly upon the ground. There was nobody there.

"What does this mean?" said Squeers, turning round with a very pale face. "Where have you hidden him?"

"I have seen nothing of him since last night," replied Nicholas.

"Come," said Squeers, evidently frightened, though he tried to look otherwise, "you won't save him this way. Where is he?"

"At the bottom of the nearest river, for all I know," answered Nicholas, in a low voice, and fixing his eyes full on the master's face.

"Curse you, what do you mean by that?" retorted Squeers in great agitation. Without waiting for a reply, he inquired of the boys whether any of them knew anything of the missing boy.

There was a general cry of anxious denial, in the midst of which one small, high voice was heard to say (as, indeed, everybody thought):

"Please, sir, I think Smike's run away, sir."

"Ha!" cried Squeers, turning sharply round; "who said that?"

"Tompkins, please, sir," answered a chorus of voices. Mr. Squeers made a dive into the crowd and caught a very small boy dressed still in his night clothes, who wondered as he was brought forward whether he was about to be punished or rewarded for the suggestion. He was not long in doubt.

"You think he has run away, do you, sir?" demanded Squeers.

"Yes, please, sir," replied the little boy.

"And what, sir," said Squeers, catching the little boy suddenly by the arms, and pulling up his nightshirt in a most skilful manner—"what reason have you to suppose that any boy would want to run away from this school? Eh, sir?"

The child raised a frightened cry by way of answer, and Mr. Squeers, throwing himself into the most favourable position for exercising his strength, beat him until the little wretch in his struggles actually rolled out of his hands, when he mercifully allowed him to roll away as best he could.

"There!" said Squeers. "Now, if any other boy thinks Smike has run away, I shall be glad to have a talk with him."

There was, of course, a deep silence, during which Nicholas showed his disgust as plainly as looks could show it.

"Well, Nickleby," said Squeers, eyeing him spitefully. "*You* think he has run away, I suppose?"

"I think it extremely likely," replied Nicholas, in a quiet manner.

"Oh, you do, do you?" said Squeers. "Perhaps you know he has?"

"I know nothing of the kind."

"He didn't tell you he was going, I suppose, did he?" said Squeers, contemptuously.

"He did not," replied Nicholas. "I am very glad he did not, for it would then have been my duty to have warned you in time."

"Which, no doubt, you would have been devilish sorry to do," said Squeers, in an insulting manner.

"I should indeed," replied Nicholas. "You express my feelings with great accuracy."

Mrs. Squeers had listened to this conversation from the bottom of the stairs; but now, losing all patience, she hastily put on her dressing-gown, and made her way to the scene of action.

"What's all this row about?" said the lady, as the boys fell off right and left, to save her the trouble of clearing the way with her bony arms. "What on earth are you talking to him for, Squeers?"

"Why, my dear," said Squeers, "the fact is that Smike is not to be found."

"Well, I know that," said the lady; "and what do you expect? If you get a crowd of proud-spirited teachers that set the young dogs rebelling, what else can you look for? Now, young man, you just have the kindness to go to the schoolroom, and take the boys with you: and don't you stir out of there till you have been given permission."

"Indeed!" said Nicholas.

"Yes, and indeed and indeed again, Mr. Impertinence," said the excited lady; "and I wouldn't keep such as you in the house another hour, if I had my way."

"Nor would you if I had mine," replied Nicholas. "Now, boys."

"Ah! Now, boys," said Mrs. Squeers, imitating as nearly as she could the voice and manner of the assistant. "Follow the leader, boys, and copy Smike if you dare. See what he'll get for himself when he is brought back; and mind, I tell you that you shall have as bad, and twice as bad, if you so much as open your mouths about him."

"If I catch him," said Squeers, "I'll beat him within an inch of his life. I am warning you, boys."

"*If* you catch him," retorted Mrs. Squeers, contemptuously; "you are sure to, you can't help it, if you go the right way to work. Come! Away with you!"

With these words Mrs. Squeers sent the boys off, and faced her husband alone.

"He is off," said Mrs. Squeers. "The cow-house and stable are locked up, so he can't be there; and he's not downstairs anywhere, for the girl has looked. He must have gone towards York, and by a public road, too."

"Why must he?" inquired Squeers.

"Stupid!" said Mrs. Squeers, angrily. "He hadn't any money, had he?"

"Never had a penny of his own in his whole life that I know of," replied Squeers.

"To be sure," said Mrs. Squeers, "and he didn't take anything to eat with him—that I'll answer for. Ha! Ha! Ha!"

"Ha! Ha! Ha!" laughed Squeers.

"Then, of course," said Mrs. S., "he must beg his way, and he could only do that on the public road."

"That's true," exclaimed Squeers, clapping his hands.

"True! Yes; but you would never have thought of it, for all that, if I hadn't said so," replied his wife. "Now, if you take our cart and go one road, and I borrow a cart and go the other, what with keeping our eyes open and asking questions, one or other of us is pretty certain to catch him."

The worthy lady's plan was adopted, and put into execution without a moment's delay. After a very hasty breakfast, and some inquiries in the village, the result of which seemed to show that he was on the right track, Squeers started out in the pony-cart, determined to find the boy and have his revenge. Shortly afterwards, Mrs. Squeers went out in another cart and another direction, taking with her a good-sized stick, several odd pieces of strong cord, and a muscular labouring-man—all in order to capture the unfortunate Smike, and bring him back.

Nicholas remained behind, greatly agitated, realising that nothing but pain and misery would be the result of the boy's flight. Death, from want and exposure to the weather, was the best that could be expected from the long-drawn-out wanderings of so poor and helpless a creature, alone and unfriended, through an unknown country. There was little, perhaps, to choose between this fate and a return to the tender mercies of the school.

Full of sympathy for the unhappy boy, he waited in restless anxiety, imagining a thousand possibilities, until the evening of the next day, when Squeers returned, alone and unsuccessful.

Another day came, and Nicholas was scarcely awake when he heard the wheels of a cart approaching the house. It stopped. The voice of Mrs. Squeers was heard, triumphantly ordering a glass of spirits for somebody, which was in itself a sufficient sign that something extraordinary had happened. Nicholas hardly dared to look out of the window; but he did so, and the very first object that met his eyes was the wretched Smike, so covered with mud, so pale and worn and wild, that, if he had not recognised his incredibly ragged garments, Nicholas might have been doubtful even then who he was.

"Lift him out," said Squeers, after he had feasted his eyes in silence upon the unhappy Smike. "Bring him in; bring him in!"

"Take care," cried Mrs. Squeers, as her husband offered his assistance. "We tied his legs together and fastened them to the cart to prevent his giving us the slip again."

With hands trembling with delight, Squeers unloosened the cord, and Smike, to all appearances more dead than alive, was brought into the house and securely locked up in a cellar, until such time as Mr. Squeers should think it convenient to operate upon him, in the presence of the whole school.

It may be a matter of surprise to some persons that Mr. and Mrs. Squeers should have taken so much trouble to recapture the boy of whom they were always complaining so loudly; but the many services of the wretched slave, if performed by anyone else, would have cost them some ten or twelve shillings a week in wages; and, in addition, all runaways from Dotheboys Hall were punished severely as an example to the other boys, fear being the only thing that would force any pupil, provided with the usual number of legs and the power of using them, to remain there.

The news that Smike had been caught and brought back in triumph ran like wild-fire through the hungry community, and expectation was on tiptoe all the morning. On tiptoe it remained, however, until afternoon, when Squeers, having refreshed himself with his dinner, and further strengthened himself by an extra drink or two, made his appearance (accompanied by his amiable wife), his face dark with severity, and in his hand a long, thin, terrifying cane, bought that morning especially for the occasion.

"Is every boy here?" asked Squeers, in a tremendous voice.

Every boy was there, but every boy was afraid to speak: so Squeers looked fiercely along the lines to assure himself, and every eye fell, and every child shrank back, as he did so.

"Each boys stays where he is," said Squeers, giving the desk his customary blow and regarding with satisfaction the universal start which it never failed to produce. "Nickleby! to your desk, sir."

It was noticed by more than one small observer that there was a very curious and unusual expression on the assistant's face; but he took his seat without opening his lips in reply. Squeers, glancing triumphantly at his assistant, and giving a look of complete tyranny at the boys, left the room, and shortly afterwards returned, dragging Smike by the collar—or rather by that bit of his jacket which was nearest the place where his collar would have been had he possessed such a decoration.

In any other place the appearance of the wretched, weary, spiritless object would have caused a murmur of pity and protest. It had some effect even there; for the lookers-on moved uneasily in their seats, and a few of the boldest dared to steal looks at each other expressive of indignation and pity.

They were lost on Squeers, however, whose gaze was fastened on the luckless Smike, as he inquired, according to custom in such cases, whether he had anything to say for himself.

"Nothing, I suppose," said Squeers, with a devilish grin.

Smike glanced round, and his eye rested for a moment on Nicholas, as if he had expected him to interfere; but Nicholas's look was fixed on his desk.

"Have you anything to say?" demanded Squeers again, giving a practice blow or two with his right arm to try its power and skill. "Stand a little out of the way, Mrs. Squeers, my dear; I've hardly got room enough."

"Spare me, sir," cried Smike.

"Oh! that's all, is it?" said Squeers. "Yes, I'll beat you within an inch of your life, and spare you then."

"I was driven to do it," said Smike, faintly, and throwing another appealing glance about him.

"Driven to do it, were you?" said Squeers. "Oh! it wasn't your fault; it was mine, I suppose—eh?"

"A nasty, ungrateful, pig-headed, obstinate, vicious dog," exclaimed Mrs. Squeers, taking Smike's head under her arm, and giving it a blow at every word; "what does he mean by that?"

"Stand aside, my dear," replied Squeers. "We'll try and find out."

Mrs. Squeers, being out of breath with her efforts, obeyed. Squeers caught the boy firmly in his grip. One desperate cut had fallen on his body; he was shrinking from the blow and giving a scream of pain. The cane was raised again, and again about to fall, when Nicholas Nickleby, suddenly starting up, cried "Stop!" in a voice that made the rafters ring.

"Who cried stop?" said Squeers, turning fiercely round.

"I," said Nicholas, stepping forward. "This must not go on."

"Must not go on!" cried Squeers, almost in a scream.

"No!" thundered Nicholas.

Completely astounded by the boldness of the interference, Squeers released his hold of Smike, and falling back a step or two, gazed upon Nicholas with looks that were absolutely frightful.

"I say, must not," repeated Nicholas, quite undaunted; "shall not. I will prevent it."

Squeers continued to gaze upon him, with his eyes starting out of his head; but astonishment had actually, for the moment, robbed him of speech.

"You have taken no notice of all my quiet interference in defence of the miserable boy," said Nicholas; "you have returned no answer to the letter in which I begged forgiveness for him, and offered to be responsible that he would remain quietly here. Don't blame me for this public interference; you have brought it upon yourself, not I."

"Sit down, beggar!" screamed Squeers, almost mad with fury, and seizing Smike as he spoke.

"Wretch," rejoined Nicholas, fiercely, "touch him if you dare! I will not stand by and see it done. My blood is up, and I have the strength of ten such men as you. Take care, for by Heaven I will not spare you, if you drive me on!"

"Stand back," cried Squeers, waving his weapon.

"I have a long list of insults to wipe out," said Nicholas, hot with passion; "and my indignation is increased by the villainous cruelties practised on helpless infancy in this evil place. Be careful; for if you raise the devil in me, the results shall fall heavily upon your own head!"

He had scarcely spoken when Squeers, in a violent outburst of fury, and with a cry like the howl of a wild beast, spat upon him, and struck him a blow across the face with his cane, which raised up a deep red mark as it was given. Smarting with the agony of the blow, and crowding into that one moment all his feelings of anger, scorn, and indignation, Nicholas sprang upon him, tore the weapon from his hands, and pinning him by the throat, beat the villain till he roared for mercy.

The boys—with the exception of Master Squeers, who, coming to his father's assistance, attacked the enemy from behind—moved neither hand nor foot; but Mrs. Squeers, with many screams for aid, hung on to the tail of her husband's coat, and tried to drag him from his infuriated attacker.

Becoming tired of the noise and row, and feeling that his arm grew weak, Nicholas put all his remaining strength into half-a-dozen finishing cuts, and threw Squeers from him with all the force he could. The violence of his fall pushed Mrs. Squeers completely over a seat nearby; and Squeers, striking his head against it in his descent, lay at his full length on the ground, white and motionless.

Having brought affairs to this happy end and made sure

Nicholas beat Mr. Squeers until he roared for mercy
(from the illustration by Phiz)

to his thorough satisfaction that Squeers was only unconscious and not dead (upon which point he had had some unpleasant doubts at first), Nicholas left Squeers's family to restore him, and retired to consider what plan he had better adopt. He looked anxiously around for Smike as he left the room, but he was nowhere to be seen.

After a brief consideration, he packed up a few clothes in a small leather suitcase, and finding that no one tried to oppose his progress, marched boldly out by the front door, and shortly afterwards turned into the road which led to Greta Bridge.

He did not travel far that afternoon, for by this time it was nearly dark, and there had been a heavy fall of snow. He stayed that night at a cottage and, rising early next morning, walked all day to Boroughbridge. Passing through that town, he came to an empty barn a couple of hundred yards from the roadside, in a warm corner of which he stretched his weary limbs and soon fell asleep.

When he awoke next morning and tried to remember his dreams, which had been all connected with his recent stay at Dotheboys Hall, he sat up, rubbed his eyes, and stared in astonishment at a motionless object a few yards in front of him.

"Smike!" cried Nicholas.

The form moved, rose, advanced, and dropped upon its knees at his feet. It was Smike indeed.

"Why do you kneel to me?" said Nicholas, hastily raising him.

"To go with you—anywhere—everywhere—to the world's end—to the churchyard grave," replied Smike, clinging to his hand. "Let me, oh, do let me! You are my home—my kind friend; take me with you, I beg you."

"I am a friend who can do little for you," said Nicholas, kindly. "How did you get here?"

He had followed, it seemed; had never lost sight of him all the way, had watched while he slept and when he stopped for food; and had feared to appear before, for fear he should be sent back. He had not intended to appear now, but Nicholas had awakened more suddenly than he looked for, and he had had no time to hide himself.

"Poor fellow!" said Nicholas. "Your hard fate denies you any friend but one, and he is nearly as poor and helpless as yourself."

"May I—may I go with you?" asked Smike, timidly. "I

will be your faithful, hard-working servant, I will indeed. I don't want any clothes," added the poor creature, drawing his rags together; "these will do very well. I only want to be near you."

"And you shall," cried Nicholas. "And the world shall treat you as it does me, till one or both of us shall leave it for a better. Come!"

With these words he fastened his burden on his shoulders, and, taking his stick in one hand, stretched out the other to his delighted companion; and so they passed out of the old barn together.

Glossary

The Glossary is of words used in this book but not appearing in *Essential English* (Books I–IV). The definitions given do not necessarily cover the complete meanings of the words, but are for the particular meanings of the word as used in this book. All definitions are within the vocabulary of *Essential English*.

Accompany [ə'kʌmpni] = to go with, to attend ; to go as a companion.
achievement [ə'tʃiːvmənt] = things successfully done.
agitate ['ædʒiteit] = to worry ; to excite ; to upset.
agitation [ædʒi'teiʃn] = worried excitement ; state of upset.
altogether [ɔːltə'geðə] = completely, wholly.
amiable ['eimiəbl] = kindly, pleasant.
apparent [ə'pærənt] = evident, clear, easily seen.
artful ['ɑːtful] = clever ; full of tricks.
assumed [ə'sjuːmd] = false ; taken for the occasion.

Beer [biə] = long alcoholic drink.
(on) behalf [bi'hɑːf] (of) = for ; in order to help.
benevolence [bi'nevələns] = kindness of heart ; desire to do good.
brimstone ['brimstən] = sulphur (a light yellow substance that burns with a blue flame and unpleasant smell). *Brimstone and treacle*= a mixture that used to be given to children as purifying medicine.
burden ['bəːdn] = a load ; a cargo ; something that is grievous.

Cane [kein] = a thin stick, often used for whipping.
cane [kein] = to beat ; to whip.
capital punishment ['kæpitl 'pʌniʃmənt] = punishment by death.
caress [kə'res] = a tender touch of affection.
caricature ['kærikə'tjuə] = grotesque, distorted (i.e. made unnatural, twisted) drawing of a person, usually for comic effect.
cautious ['kɔːʃəs] = careful (*noun*, caution).
cell [sel] = small room in a prison.
charity ['tʃæriti] = (1) kindness ; love towards fellow-men ; (2) giving to the poor.
choke [tʃouk] = to get something stuck in one's throat ; to stifle.
chorus ['kɔːrəs] = a number of people singing together ; any collection of sounds.
clap [klæp] = to strike sharply ; *to clap one's hands* = to applaud.
client ['klaiənt] = one who employs a professional man.
commit [kə'mit] = to do ; to carry out.
confined [kən'faind] = limited.

Glossary

contempt [kən'tempt] = scorn ; act of treating something as mean or worthless.

contemptuous [kən'temptjuəs] = scornful.

counsel ['kaunsəl] = one who gives advice ; one who speaks for someone in a law case.

crooked ['krukid] = bent ; not straight.

crouch [krautʃ] = to bend low ; to stoop close to the ground, as if in fear.

cunning ['kʌniŋ] = clever in trickery.

Deliberate [di'libərit] = intentionally.

delicious [di'liʃəs] = very nice tasting.

den [den] = a hiding-place for animals or thieves.

depict [di'pikt] = draw.

desert [di'zəːt] = to leave without permission ; to leave someone alone and helpless (*noun*, desertion).

devour [di'vauə] = take in greedily.

dignity ['digniti] = nobleness of mind ; a grand manner.

distinctly [dis'tiŋktli] = clearly, plainly.

distort [dis'təːt] = to twist ; to force out of natural shape (*noun*, distortion).

document ['dɔkjumənt] = a paper containing information.

dodger ['dɔdʒə] = one who avoids something ; one who escapes in a clever manner.

drag [dræg] = to draw along ; to pull roughly.

dreary ['driəri] = sorrowful, miserable, dark, and uninteresting.

Eccentric [ik'sentrik] = odd, peculiar.

elbow ['elbou] = the place where the arm bends.

emergency [i'məːdʒənsi] = an unexpected event.

emotion [i'mouʃn] = state of feeling when the mind is moved.

emphasis ['emfəsis] = force on a particular word or words.

emphatic [im'fætik] = definite, with force.

enormous [i'nɔːməs] = very big.

exhaustion [ig'zɔːstʃən] = complete, utter tiredness.

Final ['fainl] = last, conclusive.

flourishing ['flʌriʃiŋ] = being very successful.

forehead ['fɔrid] = the part of the face which extends from the eyes to the hair.

foreman ['fɔːmən] = the leader ; the chief man of the jury.

formulate ['fɔːmjuleit] = to set out in an organised form.

frown [fraun] = to look threatening or displeased by contracting the forehead (*noun*, frown).

Gaze [geiz] = to look in a fixed manner ; to stare.

generous ['dʒenərəs] = giving freely (*noun*, generosity).

gown [gaun] = outer garment ; dress worn by judges and university men.

grin [grin] = to show teeth, as in laughter or scorn (*noun*, grin).
groan [groun] = give low cries of pain.

Heel [hiːl] = the back part of the foot ; *to take to one's heels* = to run
away.
hoarse [hɔːs] = having a harsh voice ; having a sore throat, caused by
shouting.
household word ['haushould 'wəːd] = common saying or name known
to everybody.
howl [haul] = to cry like a dog or wolf ; to make a long, miserable sound
(*noun*, howl).
humiliation [hju'milieiʃn] = crushing of one's pride.
hysterical [his'terikl] = nervously upset ; excited.

Impertinent [im'pəːtinənt] = rude, interfering (*noun*, impertinence).
incapable [in'keipəbl] of = unable to.
indignant [in'dignənt] = affected with anger or scorn (*noun*, indignation
[indig'neiʃn]).
innocent ['inəsnt] = harmless, guiltless.
inscribed [in'skraibd] = written on.
instalment [in'stɑːlmənt] = one part of a story printed part by part,
daily, weekly, or monthly.
instantaneous [instən'teinjəs] = immediate ; at once.
instinctively [in'stiŋktivli] = by natural impulse.
institution [insti'tjuːʃn] = some established custom, order, etc.
instruct [in'strʌkt] = to teach ; to give orders to ; to inform (*noun*,
instruction [in'strʌkʃn] ; instructive, [in'strʌktiv]).
insularity [insju'læriti] = state of being narrow-minded ; cut off from
the current ideas of the world.
interview ['intəvju] = formal meeting and conversation between two
people.
investigate [in'vestigeit] = inquire into.
ironical [aiə'rɔnikl] = saying one thing but meaning the opposite.
irritation [iri'teiʃn] = annoyance ; irritably ['iritəbli] = in an angrily
excited manner.

Jolly ['dʒɔli] = merry, good-humoured.

Knuckle ['nʌkl] = the points where fingers join the bones of the hand.

Lawyer ['lɔːjə] = one who practises law ; one who helps on legal matters.
lecture ['lektjə] = formal talk on a set subject to a class or other audi-
ence, in order to give information.
legacy ['legəsi] = money left to a person in a will.
legislation [ledʒis'leiʃn] = law-giving.
limp [limp] = to walk irregularly, as with an injury.
link [liŋk] = connect.
listless ['listlis] = without interest in, or desire to do anything; tired.

Glossary

Magnifying ['mægnifaiiŋ] (glasses) = making larger, increasing.

mannerism ['mænərizm] = peculiarity, trick of speech, writing, behaviour, etc.

mantelpiece ['mæntlpiːs] = ornamental shelf over fireplace in front of chimney.

masterpiece ['mɑːstəpiːs] = supreme work.

matrimony ['mætriməni] = state of marriage (adj., matrimonial [mætri'mouniəl]).

mattress ['mætris] = large, flat bag filled with hair, straw, etc., for sleeping on.

mellow ['melou] = become gentle, sympathetic, wise.

mental ['mentl] = belonging to the mind.

mild [maild] = gentle, inoffensive.

miser ['maizə] = one who stores his wealth up yet is always afraid of poverty.

mistress ['mistris] = female master ; woman who governs.

monster ['mɔnstə] = large, unnatural animal.

mourner ['mɔːnə] = one who sorrows for the death of a person.

murmur ['məːmə] = speak in a low, quiet manner.

Nasty ['nɑːsti] = unpleasant, hateful.

nod [nɔd] = to make a slight bow with the head ; to show agreement by a bow of the head.

Oasis [ou'eisis] = a place in the desert where there are trees and water.

obstinacy ['ɔbstinəsi] = unyielding firmness.

obstinate ['ɔbstinit] = keeping to an opinion or purpose with great firmness.

obvious ['ɔbviəs] = plain, clear ; easily seen or understood.

occupation [ɔkju'peiʃn] = work ; act of taking possession ; business ; living ; employment.

occupy ['ɔkjupai] = to take or keep in possession ; to hold ; to take up ; to employ.

oppressed [ə'prest] = harshly treated.

Palm [pɑːm] = the inside part of the hand.

pant [pænt] = breathe hard and fast.

parson ['pɑːsn] = priest or clergyman

partner ['pɑːtnə] = part owner of a business with another person or persons.

pat [pæt] = to strike gently with the hand, often in affection.

pavement ['peivmənt] = slightly raised path on the side of the street intended only for walkers.

philosophy [fil'ɔsəfi] = study of thought ; reasoning ; exploration of things concerned with mind and matter.

plaintiff ['pleintif] = the person who brings a complaint against another to a law court.

plan [plæn] = a method carefully worked out.

plan [plæn] = to arrange beforehand.

Charles Dickens: The Writer and His Work

plunge [plʌndʒ] = go violently ; throw oneself into.
preface ['prefis] = opening remarks at the beginning of a book explain-ing why it was written, etc.
proceed [prə'siːd] = to go on ; to continue ; to move on ; to carry on.
proceeding [prə'siːdiŋ] = a happening ; an event ; one thing going on to another.
proceedings [prə'siːdiŋz] = steps taken in a law case.
promptly ['prɔmptli] = quickly ; without delay.
prosecute ['prɔsikjuːt] = to bring an accusation in court against some-one of a crime (nouns, prosecutor ['prɔsikjuːtə], prosecution, [prɔsi'kjuːʃn]).
public-house ['pʌblik'haus] = an inn ; a house of rest, food, drink, and entertainment.

Rafter ['raːftə] = a long piece of wood supporting the roof.
rear [riə] = to hold up ; to raise (rear one's head).
recent ['riːsənt] = fresh ; lately received ; of late occurrence.
retort [ri'tɔːt] = a sharp answer.
retort [ri'tɔːt] = to throw back a reply ; to answer sharply.
reviewer [ri'vjuə] = one who writes criticisms of books, films, music, etc.
ridiculous [ri'dikjuləs] = to be laughed at ; to be treated with scorn ; absurd.
roll [roul] = very small loaf of bread.
row [rau] = noisy disturbance ; trouble (adj., noisy).
rural ['ruərəl] = belonging to the country rather than the town.

Sack [sæk] = large bag made of coarse canvas for holding coal, potatoes etc.
saucepan ['sɔːspən] = a small pan for cooking liquids.
series ['siəriz] = a number of related things coming one after the other.
shed tears ['ʃed 'tiəz] = to cry.
shiver ['ʃivə] = to tremble ; to shake with cold.
shorthand ['ʃɔːthænd] = system of special signs for writing quickly.
shovel ['ʃʌvl] = a small spade for throwing coal on to the fire.
shrink [ʃrink] = to draw back, as in fear.
sigh [sai] = to take a deep breath involuntarily ; to breathe in and out as if to express sorrow.
slovenly ['slʌvənli] = untidy, careless.
sob [sɔb] = sound made when crying.
sob [sɔb] = to cry ; to weep.
spectator [spek'teitə] = a looker-on ; one who is present.
splash [splæʃ] = make water, etc., fly upwards by dropping something into it.
stall [stɔːl] = a small shop open to the street.
start [staːt] = (1) to move suddenly as if alarmed ; (2) to get up quickly (noun, start = jump) ; to give a start = to make a quick move-ment.
stepmother ['stepmʌðə] = second (or later) wife of one's father.
surpass [sə'paːs] = go beyond.

Glossary

Tap [tæp] = to strike gently ; to hit.
timid ['timid] = shy ; rather frightened.
transition [træn'siʒən] = change from one state to another.
treacle ['triːkl] = thick, sweet, sticky liquid made in producing sugar.
triumph ['traiəmf] = victory ; joy of conquest (*adj.*, triumphant).
twinkle ['twinkl] = a merry look in the eye.
type [taip] = member of a class or group with the characteristics of the
   class rather than of an individual.

Veins [veinz] = tubes in the body which carry blood to the heart from
   the extremities.
vicious ['viʃəs] = spiteful, evil.
villain ['vilən] = an evil person (*noun*, villainy ; *adj.*, villainous).
visible ['vizibl] = easily seen.

Whiskers ['wiskəz] = hair on the side of the face.
wig [wig] = false head of hair (worn by judges and other legal men).
wink [wiŋk] = to close one eye.
workhouse ['wəːkhaus] = place supported by public money for housing
   homeless poor people
wretch [retʃ] = one who is worthless or miserable.
wretched ['retʃid] = miserable from grief or anxiety.
wretchedness ['retʃidnis] = state of feeling worthless or miserable.

Yawn [jɔːn] = to open the mouth wide and involuntarily when tired or
   sleepy.